I *Survived* the Holocaust

To Share His Glory

James L. Larson

***

My mother told me all my life, "I didn't want you, you ruined my life."

There was blood everywhere, as the Gestapo dragged my father off to war. Just before he lost consciousness, he told my Jewish mother, 'get out of Germany!' He knew that the next time they would be coming for US!

We waved, and shouted, 'We love you, and we'll see you soon!' Then — at a sharp command — rapid gunfire, people screaming…people dying. The trucks sped away. My aunt's family and friends — all dead. That was the beginning of the nightmare which would last seemingly for eternity.

As I was hanging there, I knew I was going to die, I just knew it. I was so angry! I said, 'I am not going to die. They will have to kill me. I'll show them — I'm not going to die.' That was the turning point…

I looked down the street — and there was a man coming. The first thing I noticed was the rags wrapped around his feet. As he got closer, he looked familiar, 'do I know that man?' I repeated to myself, 'do I know that man? I just kept concentrating on this…soldier. He's coming closer now — then it hit me… 'that's my father!'

When we came into New York harbor…and passed the Statue of Liberty… I'll never forget that — never! People fell on their knees and cried, and prayed — lifting their arms toward heaven. There was so much hope for the future. I can't describe the feeling I had in my mind — things are going to be better now! I'm going to have a new life!

My wedding dress was hanging in the doorway. He set a match to it! He said, "that's how much I think of marrying you!"

ISBN
978-1-4602-0080-3 (Hardcover)
978-1-4602-0079-7 (Paperback)
978-1-4602-0081-0 (eBook)

Produced by:

FriesenPress
Suite 300 – 852 Fort Street
Victoria, BC, Canada V8W 1H8

www.friesenpress.com

Distributed to the trade by The Ingram Book Company

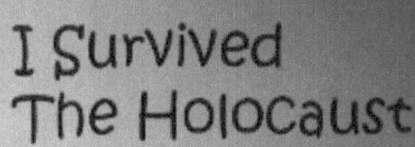

I Survived
The Holocaust

To Share His Glory

Ursula Caffee's life story

Illustration by: Gershom Wetzel

Table of Contents

Preface ix

Introduction 1

Chapter I - My Mother Said, "You Ruined My Life!" 5

Chapter II - "Jackbooted Gestapo busting through the door!" 11

Chapter III - Choose: Board the truck or stay and burn! 17

Chapter IV - "'Maybe today I will die,' – then that night I was surprised to be still alive!" 29

Chapter V - Escape from the Camp 35

Chapter VI - "Home, Sweet Home?" 41

Chapter VII - "Welcome Home Papa!" 47

Chapter VIII - Life after War 51

Chapter IX - "Going to America to get married!" 55

Chapter X - Alone on a Dock in a Strange Country 59

Chapter XI - "Here is where I'm going to take my life!" 63

Chapter XII - "Pick up your glass and drink it!' 69

Chapter XIII - "I do not love you!" 73

Chapter XIV - You gonna go see Elvis? 79

Chapter XV - I'm going to get a divorce! 81

Chapter XVI - "Don't stop anywhere until you get to Texas!" 87

Chapter XVII - Escape from Death – Again! 89

Chapter XVIII - Ted – Love of my life! 95

Chapter XIX - My Monette is gone!   105

Chapter XX - On the Lighter Side   111

Chapter XXI - Forgiveness is Freedom!   115

Conclusion   117

Final Word   119

Preface

(The following facts about the Holocaust have been excerpted in part from Wikipedia)

The Holocaust is an historical fact. Adolf Hitler and the Nazi Party were responsible for the genocide, or mass murder of approximately six million Jews throughout German-occupied territories during World War II. This was an organized, systematic state-sponsored murder of over a million Jewish children, two million Jewish women and three million Jewish men. It is believed that ten to eleven million civilians and prisoners of war were intentionally slaughtered by the Nazi regime, including Soviet civilians and prisoners of war; Polish citizens; gypsies; criminals; people with disabilities; and homosexuals.

Years before the beginning of World War II, laws were enacted with the intention of removing the Jews from German society. The persecution and genocide were carried out in stages by the enactment of the Nuremberg Laws. Most were not killed outright, but sent to concentration camps where they were forced into slave labor, which led to disease, and eventually death. As Germany advanced, conquering new territory in Eastern Europe, *Einsatzgruppen*, or specialized units, went forward murdering Jews and political opponents in mass shootings. The Germans forced Jews into overcrowded ghettos where they were confined until transported to extermination camps on freight trains. Photos are replete of these trains, as well as trucks, the gas ovens, and ditches full of people giving evidence that these events really took place, regardless of claims by Israel's enemies. Those that lived through the journey were mostly systematically killed in gas chambers, or ovens. Ditches were prepared where some were forced to lay down to be buried alive.

Incredibly, the entire German government bureaucracy was participants of this genocide program, making the Third Reich into what one Holocaust scholar has called "a genocidal state." *Parish churches* and the *Interior Ministry*, who's responsibility it was to supply birth records identifying all Jews contributed their efforts. The *Post Office* delivered the denaturalization and deportation orders. Jewish property was confiscated by the *Finance Ministry*. Jewish workers were fired from German companies and Jewish stockholders lost their investments. Jews were not allowed admittance into the universities, and those applying for degrees that they had earned were denied. Jewish instructors were fired from State-sponsored institutions. *Government transportation* moved the Jews to the concentration camps. In the camps the inmates were used as guinea pigs in drug testing by the German *pharmaceutical companies*. The ovens and crematoria were put out for construction bids with people's full knowledge of their purpose. *Government punch card machines* were used to produce very accurate records of those murdered.

Upon entering the death camps, the prisoner's personal property was confiscated, catalogued, tagged, sent to the government to be recycled and reused. Berenbaum writes that the Final Solution of the Jewish question (their description of the problem of Jews being alive!) was "in the eyes of the perpetrators ... **Germany's greatest achievement.**" The *German national banks* helped launder valuables stolen from the people through concealed accounts.

No one in Europe or Germany declared solidarity with the Jews. Neither the educational institutions, the religious community, nor professional associations stood with the Jews or spoke out against what was being done. The Wannsee Protocol makes it clear that the Nazis intended to carry their "final solution of the Jewish question" (extermination) to Britain and all the other neutral states in Europe, such as Ireland, Switzerland, Turkey, Sweden, Portugal, and Spain.

How Jewish would you have to be to qualify for this treatment? If you had three or four Jewish grandparents you were to be exterminated without exception.

One of the horrible aspects of the Nazi genocide was the extensive practice using human subjects in so-called, "medical" experiments by doctors. Dr. Josef Mengele, probably the most notorious of these physicians did experiments in Auschwitz. Some of his experiments included putting people in pressure chambers, testing drugs on them, and freezing them. He attempted to change eye color by injecting chemicals into children's eyes. He also performed various amputations and other surgeries. We will never know all that he did because the truckload of records he sent to Dr. Otmar von Verschuer at the Kaiser Wilhelm Institute was destroyed. Survivors of Mengele's experiments were almost always killed and dissected shortly afterwards.

He worked extensively with Romani children bringing them toys and sweets, and would personally take them to the gas chamber. They called him "Onkel (Uncle) Mengele." Vera Alexander was a Jewish inmate at Auschwitz who looked after 50 sets of Romani twins:

"I remember one set of twins in particular: Guido and Ina, aged about four. One day, Mengele took them away. When they returned, they were in a terrible state: they had been sewn together, back to back, like Siamese twins. Their wounds were infected and oozing pus. They screamed day and night. Then their parents—I remember the mother's name was Stella—managed to get some morphine and they killed their own children in order to end their suffering."

The early 20th century saw large growth of the welfare state with the hope that a utopia would be created, solving all social problems by developing extensive social programs. A movement of racist, social Darwinist and eugenicist world-view was spreading throughout Europe which believed that certain people are more biologically valuable than others. Anti-Semitism was not the only reason for the genocide, as after World War I the mood was disillusionment as German bureaucrats found social problems were not as easily fixed as they envisioned. The social engineering elite began believing it necessary to save the biologically "fit" while the biologically "unfit" were to be discarded. Because of economical pressure caused by the Great Depression, many began to advocate for euthanization of the "incurable." Those physically or mentally disabled could be eliminated as a cost-saving solution to free up money to be used for the curable.

Hitler did not hide his hatred of the Jews for in his book *Mein Kampf*, he exposed his intention to drive them from German's cultural, intellectual, and political life. In private, not so much in public as in 1922, he allegedly spoke more specifically when he told Major Joseph Hell, who was a journalist:

"Once I really am in power, my first and foremost task will be the annihilation of the Jews. As soon as I have the power to do so, I will have gallows built in rows—at the Caffeynplatz in Munich, for example—as many as traffic allows. Then the Jews will be hanged indiscriminately, and they will remain hanging until they stink; they will hang there as long as the principles of hygiene permit. As soon as they have been untied, the next batch will be strung up, and so on down the line, until the last Jew in Munich has been exterminated. Other cities will follow suit, precisely in this fashion, until all Germany has been completely cleansed of Jews."

Hatred of the Jews did not originate in Germany, but can be traced all the way back to Abraham, the Father of the Jews. Pharaoh in Egypt made them slaves. Haman conspired with Xerxes the Medo-Persian king to completely annihilate the Jews, and would have done it had not Queen Esther and cousin Mordecai intervened. What evil has been behind these historical events and what lies ahead for one of the tiniest of all nations?

The story you about to read is not only about an attempt to kill a 10-year old girl in Nazi Germany, but details her attempted suicide, and two additional attempts by men to kill her. Numerous diseases and afflictions have not brought her down, ***evil hasn't succeeded***. She is still alive today, by the grace of God!

I Survived the Holocaust
To Share His Glory

Ursula Caffey's life story

Introduction

The Holocaust was, in my mind, a terrible historical event far removed from my life. High School history class tends to treat past events impersonal, and in a sense, something that happened in a different world at a different time. History provides limitless stories of human tragedy and cruelty, some true and some novels of fiction. Ursula's story has affected me deeply and personally as she has shared her experiences with the pathos and reality that drew me in to re-live it with her. In the summer of 2010 there was a Divine intersection with my life and a Holocaust survivor, Ursula Caffey. Her story was so compelling that it needed to be in print, and so you are holding in your hands an in-depth account of horrific torture to a 10-year-old Jewish-German girl in 1945 Nazi Germany. This, sadly, was just the beginning of her life of trauma, disappointments, and pain. In spite of all she suffered, the joys of good times have balanced out her life, making the point that the human spirit is resilient and can triumph over all odds.

This 78-year old, 85-pound lady, and I mean a lady in the classic sense, has endured and triumphed over not only the Holocaust, but personal tragedies in her health, and family. Losing 7 of her 8 children to death, in addition to her tragic childhood and unhappy marriage became a set-up for the grace of God. In the process of drawing her story out of her memory bank, the best word I can characterize Ursula is "survivor!"

I present here Ursula's story, in her own words, as related to me during many hours of taped interviews. Over a three-year period, we met for sessions ranging from an hour to three hours at a time. I asked probing questions to prompt her memory and she began relating events many times with excruciating mental anguish. Some things had been buried, too horrific to recall and had happened so long ago that it took great effort to piece it together.

Often she would break down, weep, walk the floor, or call it a day when the details would conjure up the memory of physical pain, as well as the mental torture she endured. Memory can be our best friend, or our worst enemy. She still has, after all these years occasional nightmares leaving her devastated and traumatized. Frequently she lays, trembling in bed unable to find sleep, in a cold sweat.

"I can't go on!"

Just as we were about to finish the last few chapters, Ursula called a "time-out." Some of the most gruesome details had revived the fears and sense of reality she was re-living, bringing on flash-backs and nightmares. It culminated in a local grocery store as she was walking down an isle. She saw several Nazi soldiers approaching her as an obvious hallucination. She told me that she could no longer continue the book - that her emotions had reached the breaking point.

I had been so excited that her story would finally be out to the public, who, in my mind, desperately needed to learn of her life of victory over painful odds and how the grace of God had brought her through it all. I was now faced with a decision to press forward to satisfy my passion for the project…..or respect the wishes of my friend, Ursula. For over a year I had been drawing her story out of her, sometimes almost as emotionally draining to me, as to her. Now, all the work of putting it in print is about to be relegated to a stack of audio tapes and a number of "saved" revisions on my computer hard drive.

You know what I had to do. I had to respect her wishes. This was *her* life! I said to Ursula, "No problem, we'll put it on hold and only resume it when you are ready." She was weeping, not only because of her emotional state, but because she was aware of my disappointment and sense of much wasted time. "Please don't hate me!" was her appeal. I assured her that everything was fine and would work out in time. For about a year we kept the book on the back burner and didn't talk about it. We had contact with Ursula about every week, and I was privileged to be by her bedside in the hospital as she had heart surgery, installing more stints. She asked me to take her Social Security money around to the utility companies to pay the bills to keep them from being shut off. So many friends have brought food, clothing, and gifts, taken her to doctor's appointments, picked up prescriptions, paid bills and bought groceries. She is loved by many people who have had their hearts won over by her larger-than-life personality.

To complicate things, Ursula is battling a number of physical issues: serious heart problems with blockages; cysts on liver, and pancreas; extreme pain in knees (bone on bone); a growth on her side; and several other problems. Medications for some of these problems cause serious side effects, including terrible headaches and elevated blood pressure.

One day, after about a year, Ursula asked me to come over for a talk. Cautiously and tentatively she said she was ready to finish the book, so we resumed the recording sessions in January of 2013. These sessions were always filled with emotion -- sometimes horror, sometimes joy, but always with thankfulness for God's deliverance and faithfulness.

"I Survived the Holocaust, To Share His Glory" is not a biography that exalts a mortal, but how a ten-year old girl suffered in a German concentration camp during World War II. Over six million Jewish family members did not live to tell *their* story. This is a story of one survivor – still alive today as a testimony of God's grace and miraculous power.

I

My Mother Said,
"You Ruined My Life!"

It all started in the summer of 2010 when my wife and I were pioneering a new church in beautiful Northeast Texas. We leased a store-front suite for our little congregation on Main Street in Reno.

It was a bright, cheerful Sunday morning and we had just set out the donuts, and the aroma of fresh coffee filled our little kitchen next to the auditorium. To our surprise, in walked a thin wisp of a woman, dressed elegantly, with a glowing smile. My wife, Lois, and I fell in love with this unique, German-accented lady that first morning as we sat down with her over coffee and donuts. She was a pleasure to preach to that morning, it seemed as though she drank in every word. She joined us for lunch after the service -- and over Chinese food, I wiped tears as she related a part of her story. Such pain, such pathos!

She was back at church for mid-week service, and from that day to this, I am "Pastor Jim" to Ursula. Eventually, we merged our church named, "Resurrection" with another local church.

Her story begins with her childhood in Frankfurt Germany, just before World War II. Her mother was Jewish, her father, German - not uncommon at the time. I have tried to capture Ursula's style, idioms, vernacular, and emotional expressions, which may not always be grammatically correct.

(Ursula) "My story is presented not to bring attention to me, but to bring glory to God. I am a walking miracle, and still alive at 78 to tell my story. It's not a pretty story – it's a story of atrocities being committed of indescribable pain and horror. But, it's also a story of God's love, miracle-working power, and mercy. Through it all, Jesus was always there. Sometimes -- like now, when I reflect on those memories, I shudder as if reliving them all over again. Nightmares usually follow with unimaginable terror.

My mother struggled with many issues, which manifested in anger, violence, and irrationality. Once, when I had a seizure, which I did for many years following the war, she locked me in the closet and left the house. I had 'Grand mal' seizures, tried to climbed the walls, swallow my tongue – well, you get the picture. But……….. maybe I should go back to the beginning.

My parents both came from large families, 9 on my mother's side and 13 on my father's, so there were many cousins. My mother's mother and father were loving parents, and provided a very happy, normal home life -- but she died at a young age. My grandfather, Joseph, was a very handsome and distinguished man of great wealth, which he made in the restaurant business. When the SS (Gestapo) came, my grandfather disappeared for some time, and it was thought he went underground, working for both sides.

None in my family seemed to have had a relationship with God, but we attended church on Christmas and Easter. I had no concept of God or the Bible. Easter meant going to church and wearing hats. The hats my mother put on me were ugly, so I did not look forward to Easter – or church. My father's father was an alcoholic and very cruel. He frequently came home drunk, and misused his wife and children. She was a wonderful woman, loved by her children, but downtrodden, fearful because of her husband. They were poor, but very close to each other and their mother. He died, leaving the older children to support their mother and siblings.

My mother was obsessed with having a son, so the house was decorated for a boy. Her first pregnancy was very difficult and she almost died in childbirth. The 7-pound boy was stillborn. She was in the operating room for a long time and the doctor told my father, 'if she ever gets pregnant again, you'll lose her – see that she never gets pregnant again!' He agreed, but she wanted a boy so bad she got pregnant again - this time, with me! Surprise, no boy! She almost died again in delivery.

I was a "wanted child" but the *wrong gender*! She rejected me because I was not a boy, and refused even to feed me. She left me in the hospital, without a name! My aunt, her brother's wife, took me in for my first two years because my mother could not emotionally deal with the situation. My aunt Martha was a nurse, and already had 3 children.

I guess they loved me, I don't remember - they never showed it. My uncle never picked my up, or held me, but my aunt did and I remember that she had very soft hands! Though I was very young, they instilled in me to always do the best I can. They would say, "you can do better, Ursula." So, all my life I have tried to do my best. It was instilled in my formative years... ... at just two.

My father, Joseph, came to see me at my aunt's house. I remember the first time he picked me up. He was a working man, with large, rough hands. It was a dramatic change from my aunt's hands, but being held close against his cheek even with his course hands, was such a comfort. He would pick me up from my bassinet and speak to me and hug me. "Ursula, you are *my* little girl! I always waited for him to come and pick me up. Feeling the warmth of his body, I knew I was loved by someone. Though I was only 2 years old -- I still remember it clearly. He would come whenever he could get away from my very possessive mother. Since I didn't have a name, my aunt picked out the name, 'Ursula,' which was a common German name at the time. My father said that was fine, but my mother didn't care enough to express an opinion. My aunt Martha would kiss me on the forehead when she put me to bed, but she really didn't love me as a mother would. I was baptized as an infant as Ursula in the Lutheran Church, but my mother didn't show up for the event. My father did, and they said I was good - didn't cry or fuss. Relatives came and cake was served, the traditional food.

I didn't understand about this man that would come occasionally and pick me up - that he was my father. I had no mother that I knew, and was living with my aunt and uncle. I tried to call my aunt, 'mama,' but she said, 'I'm not your mother, your mother is ill.' I longed for my dad to come and visit me. I was really smart as a child. I would put a chair in the corner and listened to the adults - trying to figure out what they were saying. I would call out, 'Mama' or 'Mutti' in German. Aunt Martha would say, 'I'm not your mama.'

(Jim) "When did you move in with your parents?"

(Ursula) "At my second birthday, my cousins, and aunts came to help celebrate. Someone told me I would be leaving soon to go home. I thought *this* was my home, so I didn't understand and began to cry. Aunt Martha dressed me up pretty. She was a nurse, had a beautiful home and four children. The nanny and housekeeper did the domestic work as my aunt and uncle were professionals. They called me 'Mony' short for Ursula, my middle name. I didn't like my name until recently. Ursula means 'teddy bear.'

One day, my father arrived and found me crying. He picked me up and said, 'I'm taking you home to 'mama.' I was terrified because I didn't know this 'mama' nor had I ever seen her. My aunt had showed me pictures of her, but I couldn't make the connection. He said, 'your mama was very, very sick, and couldn't take care of you. She's better now, but not completely well, so don't cry and upset her. She wants to see you.' I thought, 'now I have a daddy **and** a mother.' I had beautiful clothes and shoes, and books – my aunt had provided very well. I packed everything and my Aunt said 'now look under the bed, don't leave anything.' I asked her, 'aren't I ever going to come back and see you?' She said, 'of course you will, but *that* is your real home now, with a daddy *and* a mama.'

When we arrived at my new home, I went up the steps -- and entered the kitchen. I have this picture in my head – I can see every detail. There was a window at the other end of the kitchen with a big window seat. My mother was sitting there rigid as a rod, dressed in a dark dress, and light-colored apron -- with her hair pulled back in a bun. I understood that my father loved her -- but was afraid of her. Her name was Elizabeth, and he called her Lizzi. He said, 'Look, Lizzi, who I've brought home... ......your baby!' She didn't get up. She said, **'she's not my baby!'** And that was the beginning of a horrible relationship. She didn't want me! She told me all my life, *'I didn't want you, you ruined my life.'* She continued to believe that, even after I had four children of my own. She was never able to have another child, so she never had the boy she longed for – and always resented me for it. She never hugged me, never told me she loved me. My father did. I wanted to win her over - it was a challenge and a mission -- but I never succeeded."

(Jim) At this point, Ursula broke down and wept, reliving the hurt and devastation, and a sense of defeat that she would never earn her mother's love and affection. This 'hole' in her heart became the motivation to fill it with substitutes, which never really satisfied.

(Ursula) "As I stood in front of that window seat, just barely over 2 years of age, she told me, "I didn't want you, and I don't love you, and the reason is, you destroyed my life (because she never could get pregnant again).' I blamed my father somewhat for this. For 21 years he said, 'don't make waves, don't upset mama.' Unfortunately, everything upset mama! When she saw **me** everything upset her. My father told her she couldn't ever get pregnant again because it was too dangerous, and he didn't want to lose her. She never forgave him for that.

Sometimes company would come, and I would sit in the corner, listening to the conversation. My mother never acknowledged me -- just ignored me. She had no interest in cooking, so we had a maid to do it. My mother loved to clean, though. My father was a good cook and did most of the cooking after we lost our maid. I played much with my cousins, and spent time at my aunt, Mary's. She had a daughter my age and my aunt would fix our hair, and then say, 'you two are the most beautifullest girls in the country!'

My mother was a fanatical housekeeper - nothing could be out of place. When I had a toy that hadn't been put up, she picked it up and threw it across the room. She was the most heartless, unloving woman I have ever met --and I've met some bad people in my life. How my father ever loved her is beyond me, but he did. He suffered because of her."

(Jim) "What was your school and social life like?"

(Ursula) "I was a very shy child, but smart. I would never raise my hand in class to answer questions, so my teacher would say, 'I know you know the answers to these questions, why don't you raise your hand?' I felt embarrassed, thinking I would mess up - I have the same fear today. I didn't have many school friends. We didn't have 'sleep-overs' or 'slumber parties' in those days. We did go to a nearby park to play on the equipment. I was not a popular child, absorbed in trying to figure out what would happen next in my life -- very insecure and fearful. I was afraid my mother would put me in another home, but on the other

9

hand, I knew my father wouldn't allow it. He was such a strong man in other ways, but at the same time he cow-towed to my mother.

One time, we came in for lunch at 12:15, and it wasn't ready. He simply commented, 'it's already 12:15, and we haven't even started eating.' My mother had a large sausage ring boiling on the stove. She reached down in the boiling water with her bare hands, grabbed the sausage, walker over to my father and slammed him on the head with it! All that scalding water and hot grease ran down his face as it burst on his head! She reached into that boiling water – as God is my witness - I couldn't believe it. Then she went into hysteria, and my father had to comfort *her*, and doctor *her* hand. He had blisters all over his face and neck. She didn't react to this until it was all over, and as he was applying bandages to her hand, she said to him, 'you aught to put something on your head!' This upset me tremendously."

II

"Jackbooted Gestapo busting through the door!"

(Ursula) "There was an excitement wherever this man went, a good, positive excitement due to his charisma and demeanor. He was so believable. People swooned in his presence. He was a good looking man. Who am I describing? *Adolph Hitler*!

My aunt, Helga was Jewish, and her husband, Jacob was German. He joined the Nazi's right away as he 'knew where his bread was buttered.' He joined the SS (Schutz Staffeinel) Storm Troopers, which was composed of elite German youth who could trace their Aryan heritage back 150 years. Most of them were graduates of the Hitler Youth groups who performed extremely well. They wore black shirts for identification and worked under the direction of Heinrich Himmler. Their most important function was serving as Hitler's personal body guards. Often they managed concentration and death camps.

The secret state police were called the Geheime Staatspolizei, commonly abbreviated to **Gestapo**. This group was formed when the political and intelligence sections of the Nazi Party merged. The Gestapo functioned with the SS, both under Himmler's direction, to establish concentration camps for the incarceration of the "undesirable" members of the German citizenry. This included Jews, gypsies, criminals, homosexuals, Communists, unemployed, elderly, as well as the physically disabled and the mentally retarded.

At this time, there was no internet, television, etc., so news only spread by newspaper or radio, for those who had them -- and word of mouth. When German people talked about these events, they would

11

send the children out of the room, 'go to the bathroom,' which means get out of the room. The 'bathrooms' were like an outhouse, hanging on the side of the house, furnished with a hole and a bucket of water."

(Jim) "How old were you when things started to turn bad?"

(Ursula) "I was 8 years old. Around 7 every night all window shades would be pulled down according to the law. My father had been approached several times to join the Nazi Party and the military. He refused and consequently was put on their bad list. Late one night they came. I got out of bed at the loud tramping of boots and banging on the front door. I discovered that my mother and father were already up. After forcing their way into the house – the soldiers, I think 3 or 4, told my father that he *had* to join the 'party.' He refused. There was a lot of noise, hollering and threatening. They called him really bad names, but he just stood there and defied them because of his strong beliefs."

(Jim) "How did other members of your family fare?"

(Ursula) "My uncles, who didn't resist, had it easy throughout the war as they gave in to the system without resistance. All during the war, they were protected and safe, with no damage to their family or homes. Our house was burned out by the Allies with phosphorous bombs, which took off the roof, burning everything inside leaving the brick walls standing.

They began beating my father. I don't know whether my mother clung to me because *she* needed someone or she knew *I* needed someone, for my father couldn't do anything for her or me. She was afraid, holding tightly to my hand. She knew more about what was going on than I did at this young age. These men wore uniforms and hats with the SS insignia on them. You were "special" and privileged to wear it. The SS was on the hat and the black armband, with white letters.

They pounded on the front door and because my father didn't answer right away, they busted it in. My father was wearing the traditional long nightgown, and that's what he left in. There was blood everywhere, as they dragged him out, kicking him as they went. Just before he lost consciousness, having been struck on the head, he told my mother, 'get out of Germany!' He knew that the next time they would be coming for US. I still remember the sound he uttered as he lost consciousness, just a sigh or groan. They treated my mother and I with such hatred, because we were Jewish, calling us many vile names."

(Jim) "That must have been traumatic for an eight-year old child! Did you stay in Germany?"

(Ursula) "We were overcome with fear. After the SS had invaded our home in the middle of the night, my mother made the decision to leave for Bohemia, where her sister operated a Bed and Breakfast. Bohemia was a country just East of Germany, which became Czechoslovakia in1945, and in 1993 it became known as the Czech Republic. My mother began throwing things in a satchel (we were too poor to own suitcases). The fear, uncertainty, and horror of my father being treated so brutally and dragged off were almost more than this 8-year old could bear. We didn't know what was going to happen next. I have some memory lapses - such as how we got out of the country. There was mass confusion - people screaming and hollering at each other. Everyone was pushing and shoving, trying to get onto the train. There was no communication with my family, so I didn't know their situation, but I later found out that some of my uncles joined the SS. I think one of my uncles turned us in, even though I can't prove it. We were the 'black sheep' because of my mother being a Jew. Some men with Jewish wives avoided arrest by joining up with the Nazis."

(Jim) "Did these things happen throughout your neighborhood?"

(Ursula) "I remember a whole family down the street being taken by soldiers during the day. There was a lot of commotion, so my mother went outside to see about it. There was 'fists a-flyin' and my father came out and said, 'Get back in the house!' The SS soldiers patrolled the neighborhoods every day - looking for anyone they considered 'enemies of the state.'"

(Jim) "So – you got out of Germany?"

(Ursula) "Yes, immediately. We were hungry, but didn't take time to pack any food - just a few clothes. Panic, fear, and anxiety permeated the train as we boarded. No one trusted anyone else - only looking out for themselves. People didn't even trust their own family, because many sold out to the enemy. That is what disturbed me the most - the betrayal of one's own family. Some family members had meat and 'taters' while we were starving. They wouldn't even share. Families turned against each other. You couldn't make friends with anyone - everyone was out to save his own skin. If they had a bread crust, they ate that bread crust, even if you were starving to death right in front of them! No mercy or compassion - that was all gone."

(Jim) "Is that typical of the German people at that time?"

(Ursula) "In my opinion, I don't think the German people changed after the war, maybe years later. They were selfish - they liked to control, and friendships were very hard to make. When I went back for a visit to Germany in 1978 I sensed that the people did not trust each other, even after all this time. This distrust was really unfortunate and disgusting. I spent 5 months traveling throughout Germany and observed their "macho" attitudes, especially the men. Our city was bombed out and flat. The people had been through a lot with the war, but I think they needed to make the best of it and move on. As a child, I used to love to walk through churches, where you could find people praying, but in 1978, the churches were empty, or at best, only a handful of people."

(Jim) "Wars have lasting effects on the people, and especially the Godless regime of Adolph Hitler."

(Ursula) "The people were so hard and cold in their hearts, probably due to the suffering from the war. Many Germans seemed not to get over it - not even willing to talk about it. I remember one man who came back from the war, kneeling in the church, denouncing Hitler. He described killing people. Some did this out of self-preservation at the close of the war. I had a cousin that was in the SS, who came home on furlough. Once, we were sitting around my aunt's house and she had just baked a big cherry pie (which I had never seen before). This cousin, a pilot, who was treated as a war hero told unspeakable stories of cruelty he had participated in. He returned to the war, was shot down and killed. I was glad, but the news almost killed my aunt. Then I had to deal with my guilt over wanting him dead.

To this day, I have a problem loving German people, even though I am part German. People ask me why I don't go back to Germany. I say, America is my home - I have been here for 57 years. I am not a citizen, and don't have a green card any more - just a resident of the United States. Years ago I considered applying for citizenship, but would have had to give up my German citizenship, which I was not willing to do at that time. America is **my country**. I would fight for it if I had to. I've been thinking about becoming a US citizen..... .... maybe someday."

(Jim) "So, how did you travel to Bohemia?"

(Ursula) "My mother and I spent a day or more traveling on a train with very uncomfortable wooden seats. We had no way of notifying my aunt that we were coming – no phones, and besides, we left too abruptly. Those who did have telephones had to worry that they were bugged by the Nazis. We arrived hungry and sweaty in a town, named Hirschberg, Bohemia, which is right on the border of Germany. We made the rest of the trip in a farmer's truck all the way to my Aunt Helen's house in Kinwasser.

Kinwasser had a beautiful, gorgeous setting, surrounded by mountains. I loved wading in the brook with its large rocks near the house. I went to school up a mountain, which made for a good, long walk. In the winter time, we carried our sleighs up to school, which took about an hour, and then rode them all the way home in the afternoon. My aunt lived with a man for many years, who brought into the family a girl about my age, named Ranate. I have pictures of this family, as well as pictures of my parents, but I can't look at them because it hurts too much. The pain diminishes somewhat, but never goes completely away. God has taken some memories away, but some are still there to remind me of His grace. When I have hard-to-bear issues, such as health problems, those old memories come back with excruciating pain. We stayed with my aunt there in Bohemia for about 2 years."

(Jim) "Sounds like you were happy in Bohemia, in spite of the war."

(Ursula) "Life was good at my aunt's, who was financially well off. The man of the house was kind - I liked him. She was an excellent cook, and in the evenings, we would eat our dessert out in their gazebo. My mother didn't do much – just helped her sister a little. I missed my papa, but since we were removed from the action, and somewhat isolated, life wasn't too bad. While in Bohemia, my mother got a letter from the government saying my father was missing in action. She said, 'He's not dead.' She never believed her husband was dead. She didn't want to face it. He was a good man."

III

Choose:
Board the truck or stay and burn!

(Ursula) "Things were pretty uneventful until one day my life, my future - everything changed. I wouldn't know peace for a long, long time. Bohemia's eastern side shares the Russian border. One night the Russian's, who must have been allied with the Germans at the time, came into our little town. They took over, and we were herded like cattle to a marketplace. All of a sudden military trucks with gun-carrying military, appeared in our little town. The officers informed us we had two choices: stay in Kinwasser, or mount the trucks, which were waiting on the roads at the edge of town. This was not an easy choice because they neglected to tell us where we would be going - if we mounted the trucks. My mother chose to get out of Bohemia, hoping to get back to Germany. My aunt's family and friends decided to stay. In the confusion, while being loaded into the trucks, I got separated from my mother - that was horrific in itself, not that I cared for her, but she represented the only secure or familiar anchor to me."

(Jim) "Can you remember any details of that day?"

(Ursula) "Here is what I see in my memory: There were about 3 trucks with Russian soldiers that pulled into our little town. I got separated from my mother as the soldiers were shoving, and pulling on people– just chaotic! We were given a choice, stay or get on the trucks. They were like farm trucks with very high sides, so there was no getting off if you changed your mind. If I would have stayed, I would have been killed. The soldiers herded us from our houses to a marketplace. Most of the people were local residents, unlike us who had escaped from Germany. Many of them said, 'it looks like we will be invaded, so let's get out of here!'

My mother must have thought that leaving would eventually enable us to get back home. They loaded us onto the trucks and we slowly pulled out, waving good-by to my aunt and cousin and all my friends - leaving behind the safe and beautiful 'paradise.' We waved, and shouted, 'We love you, and we'll see you soon!' Then at a sharp command - rapid gunfire, people screaming... ...people were slaughtered. The trucks sped away. My aunt's family and friends... ... now all dead. That was the beginning of the nightmare which would last seemingly for ever. It still haunts me at times.

It was a long ride, a very long ride. I was hungry - I was thirsty and wanted my mother. So, I cried. I was hit on the side of my head with the butt of a gun and soon realized that you don't cry, you don't complain. You make yourself as small as possible and you try to survive. That's the key word - survival! I did what I had to do - no matter what, because in the beginning I had hope. I wanted to live, I wanted to survive... ... but that was only in the beginning.

The roads were very rough - jostling us from one side of the truck to the other. There was nothing to hang on to, so we hung on to each other. They treated us cruelly and hard, but we thought that surely, they would take us to a better place."

(Jim) "Had you heard anything about concentration camps before?"

(Ursula) "I vaguely remember my mother talking to her sister once about camps, but they chased us children out of the room when that discussion came up, so I didn't get any details.

It seemed like it would never end. We left around noon, and when it got dark, we stopped at a compound for the night. We slept on the ground, and the next morning we were loaded onto the trucks again, and strange as it sounds I never saw my mother. After some time of travel, the trucks - one or two hours apart from each other arrived at a concentration camp."

(Jim) "How did you handle some of the necessities of life?"

(Ursula) "Well, to be perfectly blunt, when you needed to use the bathroom, you just relieved yourself whether standing in the truck, or sleeping on the ground. As I was brought up very clean, *that* part bothered me extremely. I lost all dignity, all pride, everything! I was in such a miserable state I wanted to die. But all this was not God's perfect plan. There was indescribable acts of horror to come - this was just the beginning. But, I tried my best to survive. I learned to survive the rapes - which were daily or nightly – whenever a guard took a notion. The other women, men and children underwent the same treatment.

It was a long and agonizing ride and I knew that I had arrived at my new home, surrounded by barbed wire and open space – no shelter or trees. We were assigned to little divided spaces, framed with four boards, each filled with some dirty hay about the size of one's body. That was *your* space, and you protected it because that little space was all you had left. This 'house' was your playroom, eating room, sleeping room, and bathroom. Everyone had their own "house" and you were careful not to get into some else's. Some people were mentally afflicted, and so sick in their minds that they mistakenly got into someone else's 'house.' That caused serious problems."

(Jim) "Did they ever change out your hay?"

(Ursula) "No. After awhile, your hay began to move with the insects. Bugs crawled all over me, especially during the night. This was enough to bring on the nightmares. The lack of privacy bothered me at first, but I got used to it. People see everything you do and you see everything they do. The need to survive makes you adjust to whatever is necessary. What can you do about anything? If you complain, you get shot, or even worse.

All we had for clothes was what we had on when we left Bohemia. Eventually, they just deteriorated into dirty tatters - especially due to the beatings. There was almost nothing left of our clothes. Later, a guard gave me a man's T-shirt that came down to my knees. I had no underwear, as they just ripped it off of you day or night! Those men were worse than animals!

The camp was large, stretching out a long way, and our little 'boxes' were spread out so no one was right next to you. The military guards slept in huts. I think they were assigned to do this job, and maybe had no choice. They seemed almost as miserable as we were. I'd hate to think that they chose their jobs.

After awhile, an officer felt sorry for me and moved me into his hut, where there was a cot with a thin mattress. He had a heart. He treated me fairly well. I got a kick here and there from him, but it was nothing like before that. I took whatever I got and was grateful. More about him later."

(Jim) "Did you ever get connected to your mother?"

(Ursula) "Not until the end. There were many other children and babies. Some babies and children were not with their parents, so when they cried and screamed, there was no one to console them - the guards just killed them. We had to dig trenches to dispose of the dead AND the living. If you refused to dig the trench, you went into the trench. If you just stood there, they would push you into it, to be buried with the rest. Your chance of survival depended on doing whatever was required. No matter how bad it was, you did it, just to make it through one more day!

The elderly were beaten to death - not shot to death because that was cheaper….. and more 'fun.' One day, they arranged us in a large circle, and a man shouted, 'we are going to open up the gates, and whoever gets through the gate, is free.' You can imagine the confusion and pandemonium *that* created. So, they opened the gate, and everybody surged toward the gate, and then they began mowing us down with machine guns!

These were the games they played. Another time they lined us up and made us march together, cursing us and calling us the vilest of names - profane Jewish slurs. They spit on us. They had real fire hoses that they would turn on us. The people in the front would fly through the air as the water stream struck them. A lot of people died that way. You can't imagine the extreme cruelty of these 'animals'. They weren't forced to do this - it was their 'entertainment.' It was their job to be there, but I don't think it was their job to torture us as they did."

(Jim) "Were there any non-Jews there?"

(Ursula) "Yes many. If they thought that anyone was sympathetic or friendly to the Jews - they included them. Anyone who didn't come up to Hitler's standard of 'perfection' was eradicated as inferior. Disabled people, homosexuals, and anyone not considered members of the 'master race' were weeded out. There were compounds developed where Hitler put the most intelligent, handsome and viral men, along with the most gorgeous women. They mated them together to create a 'master race.' They were all blond with blue eyes, of the Arian race."

(Jim) "Ursula, did you have any exposure to God or the Bible at this time? Since conversation was not allowed, and you had no knowledge of Christianity, what went through your mind?"

(Ursula) "Let me tell you about my 'white-haired gentleman!' Early in my camp experience, there arrived a distinguished, white-haired gentleman. They picked him up in the middle of the night, as he was still dressed in his nightgown, which went all the way to the ground. He had a Bible under his arm - I don't know how he got it in there. As he walked around the camp, he would bend down and whisper words of encouragement to different ones. I think he said to me something like, 'child, things are going to get better.' He gave people hope. The guards were furious at him and beat him mercilessly. They took his Bible and beat on it until the covers came off. It got worse and worse. One day, he was doing his 'ministry.' He didn't care what happened to him, but went to those that were in real bad shape and leaning down, laid his hand on them. That was a real no-no! Well, they got him. Oh, my God! They drug him off, and beat him up. His nightgown was covered with blood. They thrust him back toward us, almost falling down. His Bible clutched in his hands was all torn and falling apart. He raised his arms toward heaven and shouted, 'it is time!' As he raised his arms, the pages fluttered to the ground. He came toward us -- the pages continuing to fall to the ground. Then they shot him in the back! I can close my eyes and see it all again. My white-haired gentleman! A beautiful man - a beautiful man.

I didn't understand what he or his Bible was all about. Later, when I understood there was a God, and thought..... maybe that man was *God*. I saw pictures later of Jesus, with a beard, but my gentleman didn't have a beard. Maybe that was Jesus - I was confused. I thought, maybe that was the man they are talking about as God. At that time, I didn't know anything about God. I had no clue who God was. In spite of my spiritual vacuum, He never forsook me or forgot me - because I was his child and He loved me. Whether I knew Him or not, it didn't matter to God - He loved me."

(Jim) "Describe your diet in the camp."

(Ursula) "My diet consisted of a cup of warm water once a day which was supposed to be soup. God only knows what was floating in it! Sometimes we got a crust of bread, which was the outside of the loaf - dry and tough, not the soft interior. They didn't want to feed us, they wanted us to die! I'm surprised that we got *that* much. They could have just killed us, but that was too easy - not enough suffering for the Jews! They wanted to make examples of us. Many people committed suicide as a result, and many died of heart attacks. Old ladies were raped, and not always the normal way, until they died of heart attacks. I was raped several times a day and night, whenever they wanted to 'play.' This was done right in front of everyone, and you had to watch and hear the torment and pain, and there was nothing you could do."

(Jim) "What sustained you emotionally in all this inhuman treatment?"

(Ursula) "It's a miracle I'm sane - just from fear alone, not including the pain inflicted on my body. No child should have to go through something like this. But, God's guardian angels were surrounding me even though I was not even aware of it. I had no knowledge of angels or God at the time.

Later, when I went to church and found out about God, I had a real problem. 'Why did God do this to me, a 10-year-old girl?' I had a real struggle with that. At that time in my life I didn't have any help from anyone. My husband and I attended a Catholic Church, but there was no help there. We then went to a Baptist Church. I went there for 12 years, and that pastor couldn't give me any help either. I really had a hard time reconciling everything - worse than when I had no knowledge of God. After I found out there was a God and that He is a loving God, it was inconsistent with that love for what I went through. I desperately needed a pastor to explain these things to me, but he didn't. That was a really rough time for me emotionally. What, God loved everybody else, and He didn't love me? It was a mental conflict,

Now back to the camp. Regardless of night or day, they would come to play or beat me up - depending on their mood. They did their thing, I became their plaything. They even attacked the men. Oh, would they scream! Many would be dragged from their space, beaten and raped and some, after 3 to 5 days, would just die, many laid across the barbed wire fence. Without water and decent food, the people would just waste away and die. We were there to die, but our captors were in no hurry - or they would have just killed us the first day. They wanted to use us for their own evil, twisted, perverted purposes. Because they considered Jews inferior, along with homosexuals, retarded people, weak, sick or old people, they justified torturing and eliminating all undesirable people as a way of purging and purifying the race."

(Jim) "Describe the living conditions and climate."

(Ursula) "At different occasions trucks delivered more people, and once in awhile the big 'brass' would arrive - inspect, and make a report. The climate was damp, with a fine mist almost every day. I was never dry, and smelled to high heaven. Even now, I flash back to those days, 68 years ago -- I've never gotten over that. Sometimes I go out into my yard and tell myself, 'Ursula, this is *your* yard -- you're safe, there is nothing to be afraid of.' I've sat out there talking to myself many times - but those thoughts still come back. It stayed cold most of the time, and because of lack of clothing, I could never get warm. I've had cold feet ever since, even in the summer time."

(Jim) "Did you have playmates or socialize at all?"

(Ursula) "Playing with other children? Not allowed – besides, you didn't feel like playing. You had no contact with anybody, you didn't want to talk to anyone - nobody talked or made eye contact. The only noise you heard was when someone screamed. That's what drove you crazy. If someone thru out a bread crust, (so hard, you could hardly chew it) there would be a scramble and a fight to get it. If you had a chance, you just grabbed it right out of their hands."

(Jim) "Was this camp like the famous Auschwitz concentration camp?"

(Ursula) "Auschwitz was one of the three largest death camps in Germany. The camp I was at was much smaller -- more primitive. They had no gas showers, or ovens where they burned people alive. But, they were just as brutal. We had to dig trenches, and at a certain point, they made people get in these trenches, lay on top of each other in layers. When the trench was filled, we had to close these trenches, and to this day, I hear the screaming of people begging to be let out. But, you know,

God was always there with me and aware of everything that happen to me and would someday come to my rescue."

(Jim) "Ursula, how long was you imprisoned in the concentration camp?

(Ursula) "I lost track of time - not having calendars, or any events to mark time. I had my 10th birthday just before the camp and after I got out, sometime in the next year, it was my 11th birthday, so it was a little over a year. There was no celebration or party at that time because the war brought destruction, and poverty. I have a lot of things in my head, which sometimes come out that I didn't know was there. My psychiatrist told me I must have blocked out certain things, probably in a self-defense effort - triggered by current experiences. Sometimes when I get depressed, I get a flashback of something horrible. I think, 'Oh my God that really happened to me.' The doctor said that to really get cured, I would need hypnosis – but I never agreed to do that."

(Jim) "Do you think that if you could get it all out and talk about it, you'd get over it?"

(Ursula) "No, I don't think I'll ever completely get over it. You learn to live with it - it always stays with you."

(Jim) "Do you think that you could step back and view what happened to you as if it happened to someone else?"

(Ursula) "I have tried that, and I tell you, it doesn't work. I can never listen to my own testimony. Charlie, my friend and I sat down together to listen to a recent recording of my testimony that I gave at a church. I found myself imagining that it wasn't me that was talking – but someone else telling their life story. I felt that woman's pain! I sobbed for this child who never had a childhood. They took it away from her. But I didn't believe it was me. I imagined it was someone else I was listening to. It was bad, it was really bad! I listened up to the point that they hung me upside down at the camp, and then I had to shut it off - I couldn't handle any more."

(Jim) "Tell me about that experience."

(Ursula) "I'll never get that out of my mind. One day, God performed a great miracle, but first I had to go through something. It was 'fun' time at the camp for the guards. They had been drinking all day, and it was target practice times, and *people* were the targets! Some were cut on and cut up. It was a bloody mess. They took me and hung me upside down by my feet from a horizontal pole - supported by poles on each end. There was a hook like a meat hook at the top. They tied my ankles together and hooked the rope over the meat hook. Then they began whipping and beating me and doing horrible things to my body.

They wanted us dead, but they wanted even more to enjoy the torture and abuse preceding death! This was a typical example of their sadistic behavior."

(Jim) "Were they trying to get information from you, or get you to deny your religious beliefs?"

(Ursula) "No that was done at the beginning, trying to get you to tell where Jews were hidden, etc. Threats and torture succeeded in rounding up all the 'unfavorables,' especially the Jews. They would say, 'where are the Jews, where are the Jews?' People would hide the Jews, and you probably have read those stories. But now they were only interested in satisfying their thirst for cruelty and sadism. They got liquored up and made a party of it. They invented new ways of torture and rejoiced with their comrades at the pleasure it gave them.

Some people say to me, 'I never would have given in, never would have told them where Jews were, or denied my faith. I tell them never say never! You absolutely don't know what *you* would do in those circumstances. You don't know what unbearable pain will make you do. I never thought that I would say this, but, I am grateful that God let me go through this whole experience. Because out of it, I became the person I am today. I know that God was with me in all those situations.....I know that now, but not then. I had no concept of God at all."

(Jim) "What were you thinking as you were hanging by your feet, with the blood rushing to your head? Like, 'When are they going to quit hurting me? Or, am I going to die?'"

(Ursula) "You really don't think. You are so overcome with pain. All you want them to do is just stop! You moan, and scream – which only gives them more pleasure. You try to restrain yourself from reacting to the pain, as it just goads them on to do it all the more. I would make sounds that came from within, more like an agonizing groan. But, sometimes I couldn't help but scream."

(Jim) "How many soldiers participated in this?"

(Ursula) "It was like a party – maybe 20 or 30. They would all come together and whoop it up - hollering and drinking. There was always liquor present. They stood around with their arms around their 'buddies,' smoking cigarettes, and drinking - while we were in horrible pain!"

(Jim) "Did you have clothes on while hanging upside down?"

(Ursula) "No, no clothes on. You tried to replace the pieces of rags, but what's the use? They got tired of your clothes being in their way, so eventually you just stayed naked. They spit on you (which was basically a common, daily treatment) called you a 'dirty Jew,' 'Kite', and many other pejorative names. They burned me with cigarettes. Yeah, they liked that, they liked that! I felt something happening in my head. I could see myself passing out. But God was with me. I had broken bones -- but God was with me!"

(Jim) "Do you have scars from all those burn marks and whipping?"

(Ursula) "I have scars all over my body. I have three things here (motioning to her right side). I have a big hole over here (indicating right hip) where the bullet came in."

(Jim) "Bullet, how did you get a bullet?"

(Ursula) "Remember, at the beginning, when they said, 'you'll all be free when we open the gate? Well, *everybody* ran to the gate. We fell over each other, trampling each other, trying to get to that gate. Then the guards gunned us down! I got hit in my hip, and that's why I've always had so many problems there. The bullet went all the way thru, but fragments are still there, giving me pain ever since. I have three little lumps which are still there. I beep every time I go through an airport! Last winter, while in a healing revival, the evangelist prayed for me. I put my hand on my hip, and while he prayed, I prayed, 'Lord, you know the healing I need.' I went home and it hurt so badly, and then the bumps came to the surface. They are still there, but thank God I have no more pain!"

(Jim) "So, how did you live through that gunshot wound?"

(Ursula) "Oh, I eventually got over it. Of course I got infection because of the filth I lived in, but they occasionally hosed us down just to get rid of some of the stink! Somebody put some yellow powder on the wound - probably sulfur - after I got the infection. I couldn't do anything with my legs - couldn't walk. It took a long time to heal. I still have the indented scar, and many related problems all these years.

(Jim) "Well, back to the hanging incident. Did you bleed from the whipping and were any bones broken?"

(Ursula) "Yes, yes. They loved to whip you until you bled - below your belly, and between your legs. Yeah, they loved that. Then they cut me down -- no one caught me, so I hit the ground. That's when I broke my right ankle. My ankles were broken four times while at the camp, they were like toothpicks - I was just a little girl. One time, *they* didn't break it. I broke it, while attempting to run away, and in the process, I fell. It was really bad. I thought I broke my whole leg - so painful!"

(Jim) "What residual effects have you had years after your horrible experience?"

(Ursula) "Many years after the war, I discovered 4 round spots, two on my arm, and 2 on my stomach. They were holes that were being eaten from the inside - red and inflamed. My husband sent me to the doctor, who sent me to a dermatologist. He asked if I had been in contact with anything. He didn't know me or my history in Germany, and I didn't think to tell him as it had been so many years before. He did biopsies on these and discovered that these were caused by parasites. Then I told him I was in a concentration camp when I was 10 years old. He said he'd wished he knew that at the beginning. He gave me injections, and applied medicine to the areas, and after many months they cleared up. I asked the doctor if I would ever get these again, and he said he didn't know. They were little round holes that burned, and burned. When they finally healed they left a very thin skin over the top."

IV

"Maybe today I will die,'
– then that night I was surprised to be still alive!"

(Ursula continues) "As I was hanging there, I believed I was going to die, I just knew it. But that was not in God's plan. It wasn't! As I hung there in this terrible condition, all of a sudden I felt this strange warmth come over my body. Suddenly, my pain went away – I felt *no* pain. It was so amazing to me. I didn't understand how the pain left, but I know now that God reached down and picked me up and hugged me in His arms - wiping away my tears. No pain and no tears. And then (this is also a miracle) God chose one of the officers to take care of me. The man who rescued me had some kind of authority, as he had a chest full of medals.

That officer told them to cut me down and take me to his hut, but because I was so bloody and filthy they hosed me down. I had broken bones and my body was bleeding. I was such a mess. I had never seen this man before, but he must have had compassion on me. There were people everywhere. After they hosed me down, he ordered them to carry me to his hut where they covered me with a blanket."

(Jim) "Now, you're on a dirt floor with a blanket on you?"

(Ursula) "Yeah, I found that I was not wet or cold any more. The officer knew I was badly hurt. There were no basic medical supplies but he got some tape, and taped up my broken arm and ankle. He cleansed the wounds, and I think he put on some salve. Then at that point, the pain returned. I was hurting so bad I wanted to die. I was being pulled back and forth – wish to die, wish to live! I thought I couldn't take it any more. I'd think, 'maybe today I will die!' Then that night I was surprised to be still alive. There was a time when I wanted desperately to die – I thought I couldn't go through any more pain. I had a great battle with this. I said, 'I just want to die, I just want to die. I don't want any more pain.' I kept saying it over and over, but I couldn't make it happen. God had different plans though, didn't He?"

(Jim) At this point, we take a break. Ursula is replaying this experience as a monstrously graphic video – and she's the victim. She describes it as if she is not the girl, but her heart breaks for that 'other' little girl that it's happening to.

(Ursula) "Something was not right with my head, it wasn't right. The officer worked on me a long time, but the pain never subsided. I felt like everything on my body was raw. He gave me some hot water with something indescribable floating on top – I guess it was soup. Then he gave me a crust of bread. Not the soft, inside of the bread, but the dry, crusty outside.

I then got sick to my stomach, because I hadn't eaten for a long time. I didn't throw up, but was real sick to my stomach. But, you know - in my heart, I felt safe. I believed that I belonged to this officer, and nobody would touch me like *that* again.

Then I went to sleep. That's when God intervened. I know the angels were surrounding me. I know that now, but then I didn't understand - I had no concept of God or angels. Now, there is no shadow of a doubt in my mind. I know the angels were around me. I went into a deep sleep, and the pain went away! When I woke up, the pain was gone and I felt refreshed. I must have slept a long time. My wounds were still oozing liquid, but not bleeding. I had no pain. When I woke up the officer, my 'protector guard' was there.

It took a long time to recover – I was very, very sick. There were times when the pain was almost unbearable - then a warm heat covered my body. It came flooding over me. The pain went away and I was able to sleep - a deep sleep. When I woke up, I was refreshed.

One day I woke up and was not refreshed, but was angry. I was so angry! I said, 'I am not going to die here. They will have to kill me. I'll show them, I'm **not** going to die!' That was the turning point - that was the turning point. I believe God gave me that extra push, that extra strength. Whatever it was I needed at that moment, He gave it to me. I **survived** - I got better! From that day on I improved. Praise God!"

(Jim) "You stayed there and didn't go back to your little 'box.'"

(Ursula) "This officer was trying to get me healed. He didn't intend on putting me back out there. I knew that in my heart. He rarely spoke to me, but sometimes he asked if I hurt. I usually said no."

(Jim) "Why"

(Ursula) "I didn't want to give him the satisfaction. I didn't like him, even though he saved my life. But, that didn't mean I had to like him."

(Jim) "Did he abuse you in any way?"

(Ursula) "Sexually. I thought that I belonged to him. But what I endured with him was better than what I endured before, by all the men out there, night and day!"

(Jim) "Did you have any affection for him?"

(Ursula) "How could you like someone like this? But for what he did for me, I do thank the man. Like the man? No! I knew he would not send me back out *there*, I knew that, because he liked me. Sometimes at night he would sit on the floor next to me and stroke my hair and face. I just let it happen as I was a prisoner and couldn't do anything about it. He didn't beat me, but once he kicked me because I refused sex.

I thank God for sending him. He used this man, because I would have been dead by now. I know that I was already almost dead."

(Jim) "Did you have conversations with him?"

(Ursula) "We didn't have conversations. I didn't say, 'thank you for saving my life,' nor did he say, 'I'm sorry that you hurt.'"

(Jim) "He basically was just using you -- had no sympathy for you?"

(Ursula) "People like that have no morals, no honor. They are degenerates, the lowest of the low. They only concentrate on themselves - their own pleasure. And you can become like them. You get whatever food you can scrounge. It's all you, you, you. There ain't nothin' else - you don't care about anybody else. If someone dies, you look the other way. You get to the point where you don't care, you get cold on the inside, just cold.....and calloused. You think only of **you ownr** survival - **your** piece of bread, nothing else. That's how it is."

(Jim) "Well, if you don't have any desire to live, but at the same time are fighting to live, then why would you be concerned about anyone else?"

(Ursula) "Right, and that was the problem with my mother. She never switched from that. It was always about *her*. She never thought about anyone else, except maybe my father."

(Jim) "Your mother was in the same concentration camp as you, but you didn't know where, and had no contact with her?"

(Ursula) "I had no idea whether she was alive or dead, and she had no idea whether I was alive or dead. We were among thousands of people, all spread out. She told me later that she believed me to be dead."

(Jim) "You told me one time that you ate worms, is that true?"

(Ursula) "We ate everything – worms, anything eatable. If there was a bug crawling on you, you ate it. You ate it because you were starving. Have you ever been hungry, *really* hungry?

Worms - yes they mean a lot to me. It's because they are what sustained me. I probably wouldn't have made it without them. I was starving. Recently I had a fuss with Stephen, my 54 year-old son. It sounds stupid, but I'm going to say it anyway. He was going fishing recently and bought some worms. I went ballistic! I'm jealous about the worms. He said, 'you flipped out about worms?' (My kids never new anything about the details of my experiences in the camp) I didn't want him to kill the worms. They helped me - they satisfied a little bit of hunger in me. It bothers me to this day to see someone stepping on a worm."

(Jim) "Did your guard/benefactor ever inquire about your mother?"

(Ursula) "Yes, eventually he asked me how many of my people were interred. I said jut one, my mother. He asked if she was in the same camp. I said she was on the same caravan as me. He said he'd try to find her. I don't know how long that took, it seemed a long time. He did find her and she joined us in 3 or 4 days."

(Jim) "How did they locate her? How did they identify everyone?"

(Ursula) "They had records of names - not numbers like in some of the other camps. They knew who everyone was. When he found her, he put her in his hut also. He didn't like my mother, he was mean to her."

(Jim) "Your mother had mistreated you up to this time all your life. 10 years of mistreatment, but you still had affection for her?"

(Ursula) "I don't understand all that. I felt bad about what he was doing to her, I felt sorry for her. I didn't like my mother, but I had wondered what happened to her. It didn't make any difference to me, I was just curious. I was glad she was alive and I guess she was glad I was alive."

(Jim) "No hugs or kisses or anything?"

(Ursula) "No kisses, we didn't do those things. I guess we hugged. We probably expressed that we were glad the other one was still alive. We were now stuck with this guy. He was so mean to her. He hit her in the face, and I said, 'don't do that!' He said 'Why, do you want me to hit you?' So he did."

(Jim) "Why did he hit her, did she give him some back talk or something?"

(Ursula) "I don't know what he wanted, sex or whatever. She said, 'No!' and started screaming. He just slapped the life out of her."

(Jim) "Did he move her into his hut for that purpose?"

(Ursula) "Well, yes. But I think the main purpose was that he had this all planned out. He already had his orders."

V

Escape from the Camp

(Jim) "What do you mean orders? Was the camp to be moved, shut down, or what?"

(Ursula) "This camp was going to be destroyed! He knew all of this. That's why there was such an urgency to get us out - my mother and I. He sat us down and said, 'you're going to be released.' We thought, 'yeah, right!' He said, 'There's one truck, and there are a few more people getting out of here. You and your mother are going to be on this truck.' He was so urgent and said, 'we got to get you goin' we got to get you out.' I don't know if he had anything to do with selecting the others or not. He wanted us to leave, and was agitated because he couldn't locate the truck. The truck, which holds about 50 people wasn't full, maybe 40. I told my mother to just do what he says - he was so agitated."

(Jim) "Was she staying in the same hut with you?"

(Ursula) "Yes, he wanted us to stay together because he wanted us to get out together. He already had his orders, and knew what was going to happen. He told us we were going to be released. We didn't believe that -- just another trick by the Nazi's. He was so intense, so insistent. Then it happened – so quickly. Suddenly, we were on a truck along with a small group of others. They loaded us and drove out. That was the only truck that ever left that camp.

Nobody on the truck believed we were going to be free - we thought they were going to take us somewhere and kill us. The truck finally stopped and they told us to get out. We believed we were about to die! This was the end of the line and it was going to be all over. We got out, all huddled together - a lost and hurting people. The soldiers took their pistols out and some started loading them, others were already loaded. Then they started shooting up in the air around where we were standing -- without hitting any of us, and also shooting in the dirt around us, stirring up the dirt to scare us. It was more fear tactics, which they were adept at. And then they told us to run. So we ran, and they kept shooting, and we kept running."

(Jim) "Did the officer go with you on the truck?"

(Ursula) "No, he stayed back at the camp. I don't think he told them to do those dramatics. We were running, and running, and running. I lost my mother's hand. I just couldn't run any more. I was bleeding again, and my feet hurt terribly. I couldn't go any more, so I just stood there with my arms wrapped around myself! I guess I just had given up. To this day, I can still feel my arms around myself. (As Ursula is relating this, she has her arms wrapped around her thin body) I thought, 'they *did* win, after all... ... because I knew I was going to die.' I knew that! I couldn't move - I just couldn't. I heard them screaming, and my mother shouting, 'come on, come on.' But, they got farther and farther away. I couldn't go, I just stood there and... .....I know my face was wet so I know I was crying, I didn't sob, but the tears just flowed. And I said '*yes, they did win after all.....I'm going to die!*"

Then there was this weird noise coming out of me. It wasn't crying or screaming - just a whimper, and it got louder and louder, and it was coming out of *me!* I thought, 'that sounds just like the babies in the camp when they were being hurt. I was so confused, I didn't know if I thought that I was back at the camp – or if I was a baby. That was the last thing I remember – that's all I remember. The next thing I knew, I'm holding my mother's hand and running."

(Jim) "So, your mother came back for you?"

(Ursula) "No, no, she didn't come back, nobody would come back. Everybody for himself! They were too far away -- it was too dangerous. No one would even consider coming back. When I sensed the whimpers coming out of me like a baby, I just zoned out, and the next thing I knew, I was running with my mother, holding her hand. **God sent His angels** and they transported me to where my mother was. I'm now convinced of it. Some may not believe this, but that's the only explanation. I have had two other visitations by angels since, so I am convinced of it.

How did I get there? Nobody came and got me, they were too far away. Nobody did anything for anybody else. You were there to survive of die. You had no friends. So, how did I get there? I know now -- because God explained it to me later – He sent an angel!

Here we are, running, and I'm holding my mother's hand. I was in NO pain! No pain – nothing - no bleeding. Nothing hurt, and I was running like a son-of-a-gun with her! And that's when the shooting stopped. I was with my mother and all the people and I know, I know, without a shadow of a doubt He sent His angels and transported me where I needed to be at that moment. So, then there was silence. I fell to the ground. My heart was racing, and my chest was hurting. Total silence! We were listening intently. It was all over. We were free! Not really! Our minds and souls were still imprisoned in fear and anxiety over the future."

(Jim) "So, the torment was not only physical, but psychological?"

(Ursula) "We were a bunch of hurting people, in so much bondage - nobody would ever be the same again. My mother totally blocked out all of these experiences, became bitter, cold, and neurotic.

Then there was me, this little 11-year old girl. Broken in body and spirit, I was feeling so much guilt. Was I responsible somehow for all this? So many questions, so few answers. The things I had to do, along with the accompanying guilt almost ate me alive. No child should have to experience the horrific things I had experienced. It took a long time to work out all the guilt, the pain, and the anger. Why was **I** spared when so many children and babies died?"

(Jim) At this point, Ursula painfully becomes this little girl again. No one can explain how someone in her condition would experience personal guilt for what the most evil men in the world are guilty of. Dear reader, wouldn't you have loved to been able to wrap this little girl in your arms, comforting, reassuring her and protecting her from additional injury. She did not even have the basic belief that her mother missed her, loved her, or wanted her. Can you put yourself in her place?

(Ursula) "Each day, with God at my side, He guided me to further steps. They were small steps, but with His love, the healing slowly began. He gave me the power and the strength to forgive and love again. That is the biggest miracle of it all, not just to survive, but to be a human being again; a human being with dignity, pride, and self-worth. Just to have the ability to love myself, and have the power to reach out and share that love with others. I have never considered myself as a victim, but a **victor**!"

(Jim) "What did all you survivors do next?"

(Ursula) "We kept running, because we weren't absolutely sure that we were truly free. Then we stopped and listened and there was complete silence. That's when some broke down in total fear. We were in so much psychological bondage."

They didn't want to kill us, they had their orders to take us far way and turn us loose. They enjoyed the dramatics, which explains the fear tactics. We ran until we could find a hiding place. After two days, we knew we were safe, because they had stopped coming after us."

(Jim) "Did all the people make it to freedom?"

(Ursula) "Many did not make it. They were not able to run or walk. They just lay down and died. When we set out for a destination, some people said, 'just go ahead without us, we can't make it.' One man told us, 'you all go, I'm just glad that you are not in the camp any more. I have prayed that!' He then lay down and died. We lost a couple more along the way."

(Jim) All through these descriptions, and especially of the cruelty in the camp and her description of her mother's treatment of her, Ursula sobbed almost uncontrollably, and we would have to take a break from the interview)

(Ursula) "Finally, we could run no more. We were exhausted and had nothing to eat. We needed to find some food. We really weren't sure whether someone might come after us - we didn't know what might happen next. So, we hid for two days. We were still in the general area of the camp, when on the second day we saw flames and smoke coming up from the direction of the camp. There was nothing else around, like trees, or villages, so we knew the flames had to have come from the camp. My officer/protector had been insistent that we get out, and implied that something was going to happen to the camp. I know he was fond of me, even in a perverse way. I was just a 'toy' for him to play with."

(Jim) "I imagine you all were starving. Did you find anything to eat, and where did you go next?"

(Ursula) "Some people in our group knew about things growing on the ground that was safe to eat. I think they were berries. Later, I couldn't keep anything on my stomach - it would just come up. We walked the opposite direction of the camp, and travelled for days. The adults talked, but we children were completely shut out of any conversation. I was in bad shape. I don't know how many days we walked, and of course, we slept on the ground. We were pretty sure that we were safe by now. The kids that had their parents there were just going wild with their new-found freedom."

(Jim) "Do you know the name of your camp, and how many there were?"

(Ursula) "I don't know the name. There were three large, famous camps, but many relatively small camps, which is where I was.

(Jim) "How long were you out there walking?"

(Ursula) "About a month, I think. We were looking for a train, which would take us to a city where we could eventually make it home to West Germany. Two weeks after we got home, the war was over!

We came across a railroad track, and on it, a Red Cross train. The engine and all the cars had big red crosses painted on them. Our people ran - fell on the ground, kissing the train, and the tracks. There were only two men there, and they were uncoupling the engine from the cars. They said they had orders to hook up some railroad cars that were loaded with wounded soldiers at another location. We asked them for water, but they had none, but said they could drain some out of the engine. So, they got a big bucket and filled it with hot water from the engine for us. They left us there with empty cars......and a bucket of hot water. They said, 'stay close to the track and be available for the next train that may come along.' We sat in the empty cars, waiting for a long time.

Eventually a cattle-car train came along and we flagged it down. An argument ensued, and it was finally decided that we could board the cattle cars. When we climbed in, we discovered the floor was lined with people! They had been told not to stand up at any time, but lay on top of each other (we were used to that!), so we joined them, laying on top of each other. We began traveling and came to a big city, with a large harbor - it was probably Hamburg, which is in the extreme northern part of Germany."

(Jim) "Did you feel more secure, with a sense of 'family' because your mother was in this group with you? Didn't she represent some kind of security or safety for you?"

(Ursula) "No, I felt more secure and safe with the *other* people. There was just no bond there. I'm sorry - I knew she didn't like me - didn't want me. I never expected anything else from her."

(Jim) "How did you get to your next destination and how did you pay for the transportation?"

(Ursula) "We boarded another train -- one bound for Frankfurt, my home. We didn't pay, as we didn't have any money. No one was that heartless to turn us down. We looked like we had just come out of the camp. We were filthy, and ragged. My chest - my rib cage was very extended, like you see in pictures of starving people. Strangers gave us food in the train station -- a drink, or a package of cookies -- especially to me. They saw this little 57 pound skinny kid that could hardly walk - and had compassion."

VI

"Home, Sweet Home?"

(Jim) "How did the German people feel about the war, or did your eleven-year old mind have any understanding of it all? Were there people in favor of the war, and those who celebrated when it was over? Did the German people sense that they were losing the war?"

(Ursula) "Some of them were fanatical about the war, and didn't want to lose it, and others were ready for it all to be over. So, we got on another train. I remember that a lady gave me a big red apple – oh, my God! What a sight! We arrived at my home town on the same train - making many stops along the way. From the train station, we walked home, which took a couple of days. Years later Frankfurt is considered the 'sin-city of Europe.' I couldn't believe it when I went back in the 70's -- I had to be shown. The drug traffic, crime - unbelievable!"

(Jim) "Describe your house and your emotions upon seeing it."

(Ursula) "The house stood - at least the walls, which was brick. The bombs the Allies dropped did not explode - blowing things apart. They were phosphorous, which just burned the roofs off and gutted the entire inside with fire. Mama said, 'we've got to clean it out - we're going to live here.' It had no roof, and everything inside was destroyed. She wasn't that sick physically - with her it was all up in her head. I believe the reason she worked so fanatically all her life, was because of her emotional problems. The next day we started getting the charred junk out of the house. Then my aunt came and said, 'you can't stay here - come to my house.' My mother said, 'I'm not going, I'm staying here.' Well, we went to my aunt's house. That was about a week before the Allies won the war. The last two weeks was some of the heaviest bombing."

(Jim) "It's entirely possible, that the Americans burned out your house! How did you feel about that, and what do you think about it now?"

(Ursula) "It could be, and so what? People have said, 'how can you live here in the US, knowing that someone from here probably burned your house down? So, what do you want me to do, try to find out who it was?' It was *war*! When I left Germany, there were people who said, 'I can't believe you are doing this - going to a country that hurt us, made us poor.' I said, 'that has nothing to do with me and how I feel. America is my country now!' People have asked if I want to go home to Germany. I reply, 'no, I don't even want to go to visit.' They thought that to be very strange. I said, 'I have nothing over there, everything I have is here. This is my home, this is my country. If I have to fight for this country, I will. It's my country. Germany is the country I was born in, and I appreciate that. But so what? It didn't do too much for me!'"

We moved in with Aunt Gretta, but spent most of the daytime over at our house, cleaning and fixing it up. When I came out of the camp, I was 57 lbs. and couldn't walk. My mother did *one* good thing at the time. She went through a bombed-out house and pulled a stroller or carriage out of the rubble. I was too big for it, but I lay in it anyway and for three hours she pushed me until we arrived at a hospital. I think that was the only kind act she ever did for me. I spent many weeks in the hospital, seriously sick, throwing up frequently. The Allies were already throughout the hospital, so it must have been 2 or 3 weeks after I got home. There was a trail of blood behind me all the time - it was so embarrassing. She made that sacrifice - getting me to the hospital. Without that, I would have died."

(Jim) "Wasn't it strange being in a hospital with your fellow countrymen AND the foreign allied military?"

(Ursula) "I was in the hallway on a stretcher and one of the Americans – I believe he was an officer because he had so many medals. He came by with a German doctor and looked at me - and became my friend. He gave me my first ice cream! They told him not to feed me anything, because I threw everything up. But he came one night, and said through a translator, 'I have something for you.' He opened it up – it was like a little Dixie cup. He sat on my bed and spooned some into my mouth. Ah, that was soooo good….I almost ate the spoon! My first ice cream! It wasn't down 5 minutes, when up it came, all over **him**! The nurse came in and said, 'I told you not to feed her!' He was very good to me, always asking if he could do anything for me. I was afraid of uniforms at that time, but I knew I could trust him – he was a good and kink man.

The doctor said, 'the first thing we have to find out is why you are bleeding.' I could have told him! He said afterwards, 'you are hurt very bad inside and it will take more than one operation to fix it.' He also told me that I would never have children. That bothered me the most, because I wanted kids – I wanted to give them love. I had so much love to give - and no one wanted it. There were men who wanted from my body what they wanted, but no one wanted my love."

(Jim) "You thought that if you could have children, you would be able to give them the love that **you** never had. But, you felt there was nobody around you that was worthy of your love?"

(Ursula) "Nobody cared - everybody was so distracted after the war. People only thought of themselves. We applied for food stamps, and had to stand in line for hours just to get a little coffee or margarine. People couldn't concentrate on others because they were so involved with themselves. I can understand that, I don't blame anybody – except my mother. I can't see how anyone can do that to a child - I just don't understand it. The reason she became so fanatical about being clean and to be such a radical housekeeper, I think psychologically she was getting part of that out of her system."

(Jim) "So, you were in the hospital for an operation?"

(Ursula) "Yes, many - I spent several months in the hospital. When you don't have nourishment, it affects your bones. The bone in my left arm was like mush. The doctor put a brace on it and said it will take a long time to heal. 'We need to feed you good nourishment - vitamin injections, etc.' I had to learn how to walk again. I had it good in the hospital, being on a high nutrition diet. I was better off than those living in their homes in poverty. I had ten surgeries over the next few years to try to fix all my internal injuries."

(Jim) "Do you ever have 'flash-backs?"

(Ursula) "At a play the other night, while sitting in the second row, an actor in the drama was holding a gun pointing at a group of students, but in the scene, he swung the pistol around the auditorium – pointing coincidently, right at me. Then he began shooting blanks at all the students in the group. I knew it was just a drama, but it just about took me down, as the old events came back so vividly. I know the gun was just a prop, but the vision in my head was too real, and brought back the nightmares of the past."

(Jim) "What was your mother's physical condition?"

(Ursula) "My mother was undernourished, and very skinny, but not really physically ill. Her chest was extended, like mine, due to malnutrition. She was horribly scarred, and had migraine headaches. A doctor, who gave wounded soldiers injections, gave them to my mother at the base of her skull for several weeks, and her migraines went away. We never talked about the war, the camp, or anything related. My psychiatrist explained it to me later that she was neurotic. So, when she locked me in the closet during my seizures and walked away, she basically was unable to deal with it, and that was her way of coping. It reminded her of where we had been. Sometimes my tongue was hanging from right to left in seizures and she didn't do a thing for me. She closed up her mind - to her it never happened. I don't see how anybody can do that, but denial is a way some people deal with unpleasant experiences."

(Jim) "How did your mother handle the aftermath of the war?"

(Ursula) "She never talked about it. For the rest of my life, my mother never said a word about the Nazis, the concentration camp, or anything pertaining to the war. She lived in denial, and lived only for herself. She cared nothing for me. As I said, I had Grand mal seizures, due to the blows to my head in the concentration camp. She could not, or would not deal with anything except when it affected her. My seizures were connected to the camp, and since she could not deal with that, she locked me out as her way of coping. In all the visits to see me in the US after the war, there never was a conversation about the war."

(Jim) "Tell me about the rebuilding of your home and Germany in general."

(Ursula) "We still didn't have a roof, and we lived with my aunt, but my mother went early every morning to our house. She would remove rubble, and clean. She desperately wanted to live there -- maybe because she and my father had lived there for several years. She was obsessed with that. Late at night she would return to my aunt's house – they worried about her. It took a long time to rebuild the city as well as all of Germany."

VII

"Welcome Home Papa!"

(Jim) "What about your father, was he missing in action, or had he been killed in combat?"

(Ursula) "We knew nothing about whether he was dead or alive. One time in Bohemia, my mother got that letter, saying that he was missing in action, which of course she never believed. She said, 'he's coming back home!' She never explained to me what 'missing in action' meant.

One day, she found a bicycle in the rubble of a burned out house and it was ride-able! I came home from school and she had installed a large basket on it. She left a note on it saying, 'go to the market and see if you can get some food.' Sometimes the farmers had compassion and would give food to the poor. We had no money. I went from market to market and one lady asked, 'what do you want?' I said, 'is there any food I can have?' She said, 'you'll just have to wait.'

I looked down the street, toward a drug store, and there was a man coming my way. The first thing I noticed was the rags wrapped around his feet. As he got closer, he looked familiar. 'Do I know that man?' I repeated to myself, 'do I know that man?' And then the lady said, 'hey, kid, move your bike!' I just kept concentrating on this....soldier. He's coming closer now - then it hit me... .... 'that's my father!'

Then I started screaming, 'Papa, Papa!' Everybody stopped doing whatever they were doing and looked at me. The lady dropped her vegetables. I kept screaming, he kept coming, but he acted like he was really not with it. His clothes were ragged and torn, with rags on his feet. The lady next to me said, 'go to him, go to him!' So I ran to him, and by this time he was almost up to the vegetable stand. I said, 'Papa!' He just stood there. I put my hand on his arm. Then he kind of shook himself. 'Oh, my God! Ursula, Ursula,' he said, 'Ursula, Ursula!' All the people around the vegetable stand clapped and hollered. You can imagine the reunion celebration we had then! I said, 'come on, let's get some food!' I dragged him with me. I thought he was going to break my hand. The lady filled up my basket and they fastened more vegetables on behind the seat, tying it on with a rope. I had never seen so many vegetables in my life! The lady said, 'go, you don't need any more, just come down and see me again for more.' And, I did, several times…..they kept their word. In fact, one time one of the ladies gave me a hunk of bacon. She said, 'you take that to your papa.'

So, we went home. He said, 'I was so worried because I didn't know where you both were. How's mama?' I told him, 'she's ok, but she's disturbed!' He said, 'she's gonna be better…..when I get home, she'll get better.' I said, 'we gotta be careful how we do this.' He said, 'well, let's just go home.' So we went home and walked up to our big gate. About that time my mother thought she heard something outside. She had been cleaning out the ashes from the oven, and had her hands full, taking them outside. Opening the door, she immediately saw us, and threw her hands up into the air! Ashes went everywhere, and coming down all over her! She ran to him, and he ran to her – it was overwhelming!

Our house was not yet livable, so we went to the back yard. He said, 'I've got to get out of this ragged uniform.' Momma said, 'we don't have any clothes.' He said, 'do you have a piece of bread?' She said, 'no, but I can cook some vegetables.' I then went to the bakery - they knew and liked us. They noticed my excitement and asked, 'what happened, Ursula?' 'I found my daddy, I found my papa on the street! They exclaimed excitedly and came from behind the counter and hugged me. I said, 'can I have a loaf of bread?' So, they loaded me down with bread, cake, and rolls. 'Ah, you tell your Papa to come see us!'"

(Jim) "So, your father had been in a POW camp of the Allies?"

(Ursula) "Yes, they received good treatment, but they had to work hard and there was very little to eat. They dug ditches, filled them up and dug again. They had additional exercises. I thought that was wonderful. We had exercise too, we got whipped, beat on and raped!"

(Jim) "So, when the war was over, all the prisoners were released?"

(Ursula) "His was the last POW camp to be released.....it was 1948. Isn't it strange that I was at that marketplace when he came home. That was God - that was God! Why didn't I stay at the first vegetable stand? Well, I would have missed the most awesome reunion! I have been back to Germany several times since, and I always went to that area to stand by that vegetable stand and look up at that pharmacy. In my mind I can still see my dad! It's a God thing - it's a God thing.

If you look at my life - take it apart, you know that God was there, from the very first time I took a breath. I believe that my angels surround me.....I believe it in my heart! I can feel their presence with me."

VIII

Life after War

(Jim) "Now, your dad came home in 1948, when you were 13, and your house was then restored?"

(Ursula) "We lived with my aunt out of boxes until someone put a roof on our house. All we had was what people gave us. All the greenhouses were destroyed in the war. Since nurseries were my father's career, he went back into it although it took many years to build back up the business - growing plants, and accumulating what was needed. My aunt started back with the flower shop, which was a part of the family nursery business. She had to start in the back room, with tiny plants and seeds.

When my father came home from the war, he taught me many things. Whatever I know today - he taught me. He instilled in me good morals and honesty. He taught me all the good things - most of all he taught me to be a hard worker. He said, 'as long as you are honest, and not ashamed of what you do, whether cleaning toilets or doing anything else, do the best job you can and be proud of what you've done.' He instilled in me that I should be good to people, don't ever hurt people intentionally. I am very, very grateful for what he instilled in me and I will carry that with me until the day I die. He was such a good and hard-working man. My parents loved each other very much.

My father was a landscaper and florist. In my home country, when somebody dies, the family makes a plan for providing flowers, and plants in the cemetery - putting flowers on the graves at least 4 times a year, plus major displays at Christmas. He had the responsibility to care for cemeteries. In the German culture, whenever you visit someone, you take flowers and possibly a gift.

Momma stayed home, and I went to school. I began having seizures - due to epilepsy. They asked me if there was epilepsy in my family and I told them no. They examined my head and found scar tissue on my brain. They said that every time I would get excited - a good experience, or bad experience, these things in my head would get out of whack! And that's when I would have a seizure and fall down. The older I got, the worse the seizures got. It was awful. I had the first one soon after I came out of the camp – probably emotionally induced."

(Jim) "Do you think it was because they beat you on the head?"

(Ursula) "Yeah, and that's probably how the scar tissue got there. But, I know the scar tissue is no longer there, I know that! God healed me - I know when He did it. I know what He's done! My last seizure was 38 years ago. (Dear reader, you will have to wait for the details of that miracle towards the end of this book!)

All of a sudden, my mother started losing her hair. It came out gradually, in different places on her head. We all three slept in one bed, and when she woke up, there would be loose hairs on her pillow. So, when I woke up, I looked for hair on *my* pillow. She lost all her hair – totally bald! I was so afraid I was going to lose mine. I pulled on it, and nothing came out. I went to school………and began having seizures. Then my hair started falling out! I woke up one morning and there were hairs on my pillow. This time, when I pulled, hair came out in clumps and pieces. My mother then made a turban to cover up my bald head."

(Jim) "Did the other kids lose their hair?"

(Ursula) "Why should they? It was through malnutrition at the camp, that's how you lose your hair - also from cancer treatments."

(Jim) "You were the only one in your school that spent time in a concentration camp?"

(Ursula) "I was the only one in my class, yes. There were girls in my class that had been dug out of burn-out houses, but none had been in a camp. So they all made fun of me…..they wanted to see what was under the turban. Then they said I had lice! With this going on, the seizures came more often. The teacher told me that I probably would have to stay home because I was disturbing the class with my seizures. At recess one day a couple of the big girls wanted to see what was under my turban, so they ripped it off! I was totally bald.....that was really bad, I was so humiliated!"

(Jim) "You didn't have any friends that stood up for you?"

(Ursula) "No, no - I had no friends. I was so scared of everybody and every thing, I couldn't reach out to people at that time.........although I wanted to. Then the kids started yelling and screaming and laughing, and shouting, 'get it Ursula, do you want your turban, get it' as they threw it from one to the other. With all the screaming, the teacher came out and shouted at me, 'how can you expose yourself like this?' I said, 'I didn't do anything - they took my turban!' 'I don't wanna hear nothin,' she said. Then after that, she told me that I couldn't come to school any more because I was disturbing the class. So, I stayed home. I've got to give my mother credit, though - she went to school every afternoon to get my homework. I didn't have anything else to do except study - nobody to talk to. My dad was tired when he came home, and he wanted to be with mamma. She didn't have much to say to me. So, I had nothing else to do but to study. I became pretty smart."

(Jim) "So, you were basically educating yourself. You had no television, cell phones, or distractions from people. Was there a library nearby?"

(Ursula) "There were no libraries at that time. I educated myself, studied all the time. I told my mother, 'get me some books, anything to read, any kind of books.' I studied long and hard. I wanted to be a doctor. I had the grades - I could have gone into medical school. My father said, 'The business we have.....you are the only one.' My father wanted me to continue in the family business. He took care of the cemetery landscaping and my aunt took the florist part of the business. I said, 'I want to be a doctor.' He said, 'Ill make a deal with you. You start flower designing school, and go 6 months and see how you like it.'

Flower design is a big deal in Europe - not like here. You have to complete three years of school and then pass a State exam. You go 6 weeks here in America and call yourself a designer. He said if you absolutely don't like it – ok, we'll talk. I started designer school at age 16, along with my regular school work that I was doing at home. I loved it! When I went to designing school, I told them, 'I have seizures, I'm an epileptic.' The master said, 'ok, when you have a seizure, what do you want me to do?' He was cool. He was an older man - really neat. I gave him my tongue depressors and told him, 'stick this in my mouth so I won't swallow my tongue, and the seizure usually will go away after awhile. I'll probably end up on the floor.' He said, 'Ok, we can handle it!' Surprisingly, I had very few seizures there. I felt comfortable... ...I knew that if I have one there it would be all right. I had some at home, but very few at designer school. The teachers loved me, and cut up with me. I had wonderful grades, and I loved hands-on work. I worked with my aunt, which I enjoyed. I thought, well, this is what my dad wants me to do, so I'll go ahead and do it. It's a very tough 3-year course. There were write-ups in the local paper on my work. Flowers in Germany were very important. Birthday parties may not always have gifts, but they definitely had flowers - I even wore flowers in my hair. When you went visiting, you always took flowers, and I do that even today!"

(Jim) Whenever Ursula comes to my house for a visit, she always brings a fresh flower arrangement she has made!

(Ursula) "I've always been sorry that I didn't go to medical school. It probably would have hurt my dad. But, I had a nice career... ...I really did. I had my own shop, and I worked in other fine shops. I learned a lot throughout the years. In European, designing was a unique profession - in high demand. I'm not sorry that I became a flower designer... ... ...I'm just sorry that I didn't stand up for myself! I should have said, 'I want to become a doctor and that's what I'm going to do!' Without being ugly, I should have insisted on my dream - to help people."

(Jim) "Maybe when you get to heaven, God will let you be a doctor."

(Ursula) (Laughing) "They won't need doctors then, there will be no sickness!"

IX

"Going to America to get married!"

(Ursula) "When I was 16 I met a boy named Rudy Recham. My parents objected to him because he came from a divorced home - and from the 'wrong side of the tracks.' He rode a motorcycle, wore a leather jacket, leather pants, and to finish it off - had long hair. That was not done in those days, not in Germany. So he was a 'bad' boy, he really was, especially in my parent's eyes. He was my first love! The more they rejected him, the more I rebelled. That was the first time I showed any hostility towards my parents - even towards my mother. I was never mean to my mother, but my attitude at that time was, 'I'm goin' to do it, no matter what anyone says.'

Rudy and I got engaged when I was 18. I went camping a lot with a group of friends. Rudy, at 22 was also a part of that group. He played the guitar and sang beautifully. We had tents, and spent a lot of time camping out. My parents had checked the situation out and approved. He was a wonderful young man – assuring me that he loved me. There was no violence, no ugliness or anything – he was gentle with me. His mother had been divorced and remarried a German/American, who was stationed in Germany and had a very good job.

His parents decided to return to America, and Rudy wanted to return with them. Rudy was the only son, but had two older sisters. His mother didn't like me very much. She thought that if they all moved to America, our relationship would fade away. We had a beautiful engagement party and in a few months Rudy left for America with his family. We wrote frequently, reaffirming our love for each other. He never let on that our relationship had changed. He left for America, promising me he would get a job, and send me the money to come over - then we would get married. I had my wedding gown, and my trousseau. In those years I accumulated what I would need for my home. I received as gifts, tablecloths, cloth napkins, dishes, kettles – everything to set up housekeeping. Every birthday and Christmas provided more things for my new marriage."

(Jim) Ursula suddenly begins to weep as a very painful memory surges up to her consciousness that had been suppressed for many years. I waited patiently for her to regain her composure to go on.

(Ursula) "Pastor Jim, what I'm about to tell you is something I've never disclosed to anyone. I am so ashamed and embarrassed to have to tell you about my first pregnancy. Rudy and I… … … …..well, a few months after he left for America, I realized that I was pregnant. When my mother found out she lost all control. She began screaming at me and kicking me in the stomach to the point that I miscarried! This was one of the most painful experiences of my life. How could a mother treat a daughter so cruelly? My greatest desire in my whole life has been to be a good, loving mother to my children."

(Jim) "This must have put a serious strain on family relationship from this point on!"

(Ursula) "Yes, but as time goes on, you adjust, recover, and go on with life. I was still determined to marry Rudy, for what I felt for him, and what I thought he felt for me was bigger than life.

I could not leave without my parent's permission until I was 21, and Rudy said that was fine. We got large shipping crates, lined the inside with metal so that all my belongings and home-making things would be protected on the ship. I packed up everything, and wrote to tell him I would soon be 21 and ready to come - please send the fare money. I told my family that I was going even though they put up a fuss. They thought I would get over the desire with the passing of time and change my mind. That didn't happen."

(Jim) "What did you know of America, and was your attitude positive or negative."

(Ursula) "Outside of a cousin who married an American, and the American military presence around me, I knew very little, because they only spoke English, which I could not understand. I had not studied their culture or read anything about America."

(Jim) "You were willing to leave for a strange country - a country that had conquered your home country, Germany -- all for the love of Rudy?"

(Ursula) "Yes. I thought that I could leave all the bad memories of my childhood and the concentration camp behind me and start a new life. I couldn't wait to leave. I didn't realize that all my problems - all my issues went right with me on that boat."

(Jim) "Did Rudy have a job or career in America?"

(Ursula) "Yes, he was a chemist - made good money. He could have had a wonderful career. My parents went with me to Hamburg to board an Italian ship, named 'Italia.'"

It took two weeks for the trip. I was in third class, with 3 other women. We only went into our tiny cabin to sleep – spending the rest of the time on deck. I had a wonderful time on the ship – met some nice people!"

(Jim) "Who were your fellow passengers - business people, vacationers?"

(Ursula) "No, they were immigrants. Everyone was headed to America with great hope - to start a new life. I didn't get sea sick, not one day. I sat at the Captain's table frequently, because I was one of the few that didn't get sick."

(Jim) "Were all those on the ship Germans?"

(Ursula) "Oh no, they were from all over - many countries. Everybody wanted to get away from where they were from – to start anew. This was a ship full of very poor immigrants - owning only the clothes they had on. The captain, the staff, and the food were outstanding. I never ate so well! They took good care of everyone. Often we saw sharks, and whales following us along side of the ship. Porpoises jumped out of the water – putting on a show for us. I was on the deck all the time – they had to call me below every night. The water was fascinating to me – just like in the movies."

(Jim) Here, Ursula transports herself back to a very rare, but happy time in her life. No doubt she had joyful anticipation of being a new bride, escaping the horrible memories of the war, and relieved to leave a mother who became a constant reminder of rejection and disappointment. She was like a little child on board with new, exciting, experiences, and enjoyed meeting people from many parts of the world. Everyone's relief of the war being over and the anticipation of a new life in America must have been a source of hope and excitement.

(Ursula) "It was not an elegant, modern cruise ship like today's ocean liners - but an old ship. Just before we arrived, the captain asked if anyone wanted to send a telegram to someone in New York so they could meet them at the dock. I said that I would, and sent a telegram to Rudy. Our arrival was to be May 16, at 9:30 in the morning. Finally, the captain announced that he wanted everyone to come to the main deck and watch as we were about to come into the New York harbor. He said, 'everyone look to the right.' Then we came in... ...and passed the Statue of Liberty... .....I'll never forget that -- never! People fell on their knees and cried, and prayed – lifting their arms toward heaven. There was so much hope for the future. I can't describe the feeling I had -- things are going to be better now! I'm going to have a new life. I'm going to have a new life! I'm going to have a new life, all right! (sarcastically, thinking back)"

X

Alone on a Dock in a Strange Country

(Ursula) "We arrived and there was **no one** to meet me! I wasn't too worried at first - I thought they were just running a little late. I had heard about New York City - the crowds, the taxis, the traffic – so many things that might cause the delay. I was sitting by myself, surrounded by all my trunks, bags, and suitcases. The crates containing all my house ware items were in transit and would arrive later.

There I sat, surrounded with baggage – just 'a-bawlin.' I sat there all day – until dark and still no one came. A man who worked on the docks came up to me and knowing that I had gotten off the last ship, tried to communicate with me. He couldn't speak German, and I couldn't speak English. He found someone who could speak some Hebrew. I showed him the letter from Rudy, with the address, and said 'that's where I need to go.' Rudy always included his phone number on every letter. The man kept checking on me, and once brought me a cup of coffee. He went to call and upon returning said there was no answer.

They finally arrived around 9:30 that night, 12 hours late. Rudy came, along with his mother and step-father. It was a very cold greeting. His mother said, 'I didn't know you were already here.' She *knew* when I was coming - exactly the time and the date, plus they had received my telegram. Rudy said, 'I'm so happy you are here, I've waited so long!' In the moment of that excitement, I didn't know anything except that I was so excited to see him, and for him to hold me in his arms. I didn't know that he had changed!

We then went to their apartment nearby in New Jersey, which was very nice. His mother asked me if I was hungry - of course, I was starving, not haven't eaten since leaving the ship! Rudy and I went into his bedroom and talked about our future and we seemed happy together. He said he had a job, and told me that I would have to get a job. 'The best job you can get is to work in people's homes - cleaning.' I said, 'why should I do that, I have a profession as a floral designer?' I had every certificate you could get – that's how good I was. I thought that would mean something, but apparently, that doesn't mean anything in America. I said, 'I don't mind working in houses, but why can't I work in my profession?' He said, 'I think because you don't speak English, it would be hard for you to work in that profession.' We let it go and didn't talk about it for awhile. His mother worked in homes, and she said she made good money – 'and that's what you need to do,' she said.

I said, 'I worked all these years to learn this profession and be good at it. I don't mind cleaning houses, but I'd rather work in my profession.' Rudy left the house every morning between 6:30 and 7:00 for work. He got home later and later every night that first week - there was always some excuse. Then I noticed little things, personal things that made me suspicious. I watched his mother closely - she did not care for me one little bit. She told me, 'I don't think this was a good idea, you coming over here from Germany.' I said, 'Rudy wanted me to come, he wanted us to get married!' She said, 'well, he has made other plans.' I said, 'Well, he didn't tell *me* about any other plans. All he said was he wanted me to work in houses.'

Finally, one night, about two weeks after I arrived, things came to a head - been going downhill fast. My father had given me $300 which I gave Rudy on the first night. I told him that this was from my dad - he gave it to us for our wedding. He took the money – that was ok, we were going to get married – that was for both of us. I trusted him. But, after two weeks, I began to disbelieve some of the things he said. He told me that he was going into the military. I told him that I didn't understand how someone from Germany could go into the US service, and *why* would he want to do that. He said he was unhappy with his job. I asked him why he didn't find another job. He told me that I needed to go clean houses, and he'd go into the service. He said we'd save our money, and then we would get married. I said, 'but you told me that we would get married – I want to get married now! I don't want to sleep with you, and not be married – don't make me do that.'"

(Jim) "You mean, he wanted you both to live like married people and not get married, and then be separated while he was off in the military?'

(Ursula) "I guess. I couldn't believe his behavior. Then he said, 'you know what? You have changed too much, I'm not going to get married – I'm not going to marry you!'

It went on and on, and then his mother told me, 'who are you to make demands on him, he has someone in New York, a widow, where he has been going every night!' She said that I must be really dumb! My wedding dress was hanging in the doorway. (Ursula begins to weep as the memories rush back). He lit a match to it! He said, 'that's how much I think of getting married!"

(Jim) "He and his mother just stood there and watched it burn?"

(Ursula) "She was in the kitchen and didn't care one way or another. Why would she care about a wedding dress? She didn't care about *me* as a person, why would she care about my wedding dress? It was satin, and just went up in flames instantly. I had hung it in a large arched doorway, so as to not get wrinkled - I didn't have a closet. I hung it up there because I thought I was going to get married in the next couple of days. When it was about half burned, he stuffed the remaining charred remains into a trash can and put water on it."

(Jim) "Was there ever any physical abuse by Rudy - had he ever struck you?"

(Ursula) "Back in Germany, he once hit me in the face. He was taking me home from a movie - I don't know what transpired, but he got real angry with me. We were walking up the stairs to my house and he slapped my face. My father was just coming out and saw it happen. My father got a hold of him – he didn't hit him, but he told him, 'if you ever touch my daughter again, you will have to deal with me.' At that time I believed Rudy was a fine man - I don't know why he hit me that night. We had a pleasant time at the movie, so I didn't understand his behavior. He apologized and said it would not happen again, and it never did.

In the mean-time, my trunks arrived. All the houses and apartments in that area had cellars, so that's where they put my trunks. It was a three-story apartment and each floor had a section in the cellar for storage. He told me it was over and I had to get out! His mother said, 'you have to get out – you can't stay here!' Before I left, Rudy went down to the cellar, and used a tire iron to burst open the crates – and then proceeded to smash all my dishes and everything in the trunks!"

(Jim) "Why did he destroy all your stuff?"

(Ursula) "Why did he let me come all the way from Germany? That's the big question! I think that he was on drugs. He did drink a lot, but since there was such a change in him, I believe drugs were involved. When I arrived, I didn't see all this – I was just so happy to see him! He was a totally different person. His step-father was not involved, and paid no attention. Why would anyone want to put someone through this - telling me in his letters how much he loved me! I know that at one time he *did* love me – no one can take that away from me! Maybe his mother had something to do with it, or maybe it was drugs. The whole thing doesn't make sense."

XI

"Here is where I'm going to take my life!"

(Jim) "So, you were kicked out of their house?"

(Ursula) "Yes, I left the house and I walked... ... ...and walked. I was in New Jersey, and ended up close by in New York -- but I don't know how I got there."

(Jim) "Did you take any luggage with you?"

(Ursula) "I took nothing, only my purse. There was such chaos, screaming, and I was crying – probably hysterical. They said, 'get out, get out!' I just grabbed my purse and left all my luggage, clothes, and makeup I didn't even think - it didn't make sense to take anything – I didn't even know where I was going. How could anybody do that – bringing someone to a strange country, who doesn't even speak the language?"

(Jim) "Did you have any money?"

(Ursula) "No, Rudy had taken all my money. I trusted him at the first when he said he would take care of it. I was totally shocked, confused and panicked. I walked and walked in New York City, thinking, 'what am I going to do, where am I going to go?' I always carry a little comb with me, even today. I had an empty purse, except for that little comb. I left the streets and arrived at a park."

(Jim) "So, let me get the picture. You are now walking, not knowing where you are going. You have no money, and know absolutely no one. You are crying because you are thousands of miles away from home, having lost everything you own. Your whole world has just come down on you!"

(Ursula) "That's the sad truth. I was in a strange country, not knowing the language, and broke. I just kept walking. My feet were killing me - I was scared, and hungry. So many people…… …..I was so frightened! I came to a park with a lot of trees and benches, which seemed safer than the streets. I lied down on a bench, with my purse under my head – I guess I went to sleep."

(Jim) "What did you think when you woke up, and how did you plan to get out of this situation?"

(Ursula) "I thought, 'what am I going to do tomorrow? I can't sleep here forever.' I was hoping someone would find me. It was early June and the nights were cool. I got cold in the night, and woke up in the morning in pain. I spent much time sobbing. I blamed myself saying, 'why did I come - I should have listened to my parents, I should have stayed home!' I walked some more, looking for something to eat. I saw some berries, but was afraid to eat them. I just kept walking - hoping someone would find me. I had gotten to a place where there were no people around – it was like someone had come along and swept every-one out. I then found an even more deserted park near a river, where there were some benches. I stayed there because I was afraid of walking the streets again. I found some mushrooms, but was afraid they might be poisonous, so didn't eat them. I did not see a soul. I was so hungry!"

(Jim) "I imagine your mind was just whirling, trying to figure out what you should do next."

(Ursula) "Yeah, and if I found somebody, how would I make myself understood? What am I going to tell them, 'I have nowhere to go!' I thought, if I could get someone to understand me, maybe I could get them to contact my father in Germany so he could wire me some money to come back home. But, I wasn't going to do that – even if I had to die, I was **not** going to do that. I was not going to admit that I was wrong and they were right – I was not going to do that! I went through too much -- I was not going to bring more shame on my family. Everyone believed, 'Ursula is going to America – to get married!' And then it would be said, 'Ursula is going to come home?' No way, no way!"

(Jim) "So, you slept on that same bench and saw no people?"

(Ursula) "Right, there was no one around. I came to the point that I believed I had no other solution but to take my life. What am I going to do - sleep in the park until I starve to death – or somebody find me in the mean time and rape me? I wasn't going to go through any more of that stuff – that was all over! I came to that point – that's a hard decision to make. That was a terrible situation. I felt I had no other choice. Maybe I could have gone back on the street – I don't know. To me that was it – I'm not going to suffer any more, not going to be hungry any more, not going to be cold any more -- it's going to finally be all over! I was so involved with my own pain and problems I just needed to find a way to survive again. But I was just so tired of surviving over and over. So, I just gave up! Maybe I could have found somebody that would understand me or listen to me, but I was too tired, too proud and didn't want to deal with it anymore. That's what I had tried to do all my life – **survive**! I just had enough of it. (She's weeping again).

On the fourth day, I made up my mind. There was nothing left to do – I was going to take my life – that was the simplest way. I walked around the area, looking for a place in the river to do it. I found it. I went back to my bench, struggling with my decision. Later on that night I went back to the spot I had picked out. It was rocky and deep, with a place from which I could jump. I knew it was going to be over soon!"

(Jim) "Could you swim?"

(Ursula) "Yes, I am a good swimmer, but I didn't *want* to swim – I wanted to die. I wanted to get rid of the pain and all that stuff! So, it got dark and I found the place. I stood there, looking into the sky. I asked my parents to forgive me for the shame I was bringing on them. I am killing myself! I told them I loved them – even my mother! Then it was so quiet – I didn't hear a sound. It was so, so quiet, even eerie. It was dark, but… ……*all of a sudden*, I could see a cloud formation like a circle in front of me. Then, Jesus' face appeared in the cloud! I didn't know for sure at the time it was Jesus, but I knew it was something supernatural, so I assumed it was Jesus! This face appearance was not something you would see every day. As His face appeared, his eyes were fascinating. Then He held up His hand like a gesture of, 'Stop!' 'Stop!' I said, 'Who are you?' I fell on my knees and cried, and I cried, and I looked up -- He was still there! The cloud formation swirled around – then it was gone!"

(Jim) "Was the image inside the cloud?"

(Ursula) "Yes, inside the cloud formation. His eyes were a brilliant blue - just beautiful! And piercing! I fell to the ground, sobbing and crying, and speaking German. I didn't know the meaning exactly. I said to myself, 'what happened?' But… …… I knew then I didn't want to die – I knew that – I didn't want to die anymore! Suddenly a police cruiser drove up. I hadn't seen a person or vehicle in three days! They thought I was hurt - thought I had been raped. They talked to me in English, I talked back in German. I was hysterical and motioning to the sky. I told them in German that I saw 'Jesus' in the cloud. I had seen pictures of Jesus, and this looked like those pictures. But, I had never seen in those pictures the brilliance of those eyes. I kept saying to them, 'Jesus, Jesus.' They just said one word, 'Belleview' which is a famous New York mental hospital! They then loaded me into the cruiser, and began talking to each other about taking me to the police station. At the station, they found a little Jewish man that I could communicate somewhat. That's when I got my first American *hamburger and French fries*!"

(Jim) "Did they take you to a restaurant?"

(Ursula) "No, they brought it into the police station. I was in no condition to go anywhere - you should have seen how filthy I was! Maybe that's why I am so strict about cleanliness today -- I almost scrub my skin off! They brought me a hamburger and French fries – wow, what a sight! That's not something we had in Germany. I woofed it right down -- and threw it right back up. I hadn't eaten for so long, and I ate it too fast. My stomach was a bundle of nerves."

(Jim) "You were able to communicate with the little Jewish man?"

(Ursula) "We did what we could. He knew my name was Ursula, that I came on a ship from Germany, and that I was 21 years old. The hardest part to get across was why I was on the street – and where was I going. I don't think they completely understood – *I* didn't understand!"

(Jim) "Were you always about the same size as you are now?" (85 pounds!)

(Ursula) "No, I always stayed right at 125 pounds -- until the last few years. Well, they all talked and decided that the little Jewish man would take me home with him to his wife. They were older, around 60. He must have called her, because she was baking a pie and met us at the door. She hugged me, wrapped her arms around me and I think she said, 'you poor little child!' She took me into the house and asked me if I was hungry. My stomach was in bad shape. He told her that I had thrown up. There were a lot of hand motions, enhancing the communication. She took me into the bathroom, turned on the tub faucet and said I might want to take a bath. She added bubble bath and made me get into the tub. 'Oh, what a pleasure!' When I was done, she came and dried me off, just like I was a child – she knew what I needed – and she gave it to me. It was wonderful! I was very, very needy, and that woman knew it. Then she indicated that we would talk more tomorrow, and she tucked me into bed.

The next afternoon, while watching soap operas – she put a stool between her legs and had me sit on it. She wrapped her arms around from the back and held me, and just talked and talked to me in a soft voice. I would even drop off to sleep - it felt so good. Sometimes when I cried a lot, she would make me come to her lap, stroke my hair, and pat my arms. She was a very intelligent woman – she knew I was in bad shape and sensed what I needed and supplied it. She ministered to me emotionally."

(Jim) "How long did you stay with the policeman and his wife?"

(Ursula) "About six weeks. I had to get my strength back, as I had not eaten for four days. She fed me light things, like oatmeal, so I ate a lot of oatmeal, and to this day, I don't like oatmeal! She held up an egg and tried in sign language to ask me how I wanted it fixed. It was so funny! I even got better up in my head! There was no way now that I could ever commit suicide. After seeing Jesus in that cloud, there was no way I wanted to die – no way, that was all over with. No one could ever get me to that place again!"

XII

"Pick up your glass and drink it!"

(Jim) "Were you pretty much recovered then and ready to strike out on your own?"

(Ursula) "It was time to look for a job. The policeman and his wife didn't want me to get a job yet, but I felt I was ready. She coached me as what to say. She taught me to ask, 'are you hiring?' It was just a few words, so I thought I could remember them. There was only one flower shop in the area. I kept rehearsing in my head over and over, 'are you hiring?' I walked into the flower shop, and got so nervous I forgot what to say! A man came out and asked me, 'can I help you?' I said, 'yeah – do you like me?' That stumped him! He then called out his brother (they were partners) and asked him, 'do you like her?' They seemed amused at me, but they eventually figured out that I was asking for a job. They said 'yes, can you come tomorrow?' I said, 'yes' and was excited about my new job."

(Jim) "How much did they pay you?"

(Ursula) "$39 a week, including Saturdays. But I did so well, they put me out on the street with buckets of flowers. I got 10 percent of those sales in addition. I was at a bus stop and there was a lot of people-traffic - so I did well. I eventually got a raise. My bosses were extremely good to me - even their wives. They helped me get a little apartment costing $50 a month. They took me to places like the Empire State Building, and Radio City. They picked me up for work in the morning and dropped me off in the evening. They really loved me - was so good to me – even bought me a TV. They included me in all their family gatherings, such as holidays. They were Greek, and had big families – with big meals. I loved their parents, and their kids – it was one big happy family! I always cherished those two brothers. They respected me as a person and never did anything inappropriate.

(Jim) "Whatever happened to Rudy? Did you hear anything from him?"

(Ursula) "I heard that he returned to Germany. He thought that I had gone back to Germany, and was looking for me and went to see my parents. He begged them, 'please, tell me where Ursula is.'

Months later I arrived to my little home one evening – and had an eerie feeling. I didn't see anything unusual, but it felt funny. My apartment was just a kitchen and a bedroom, separated by a curtain. All of a sudden, Rudy came out from the other side of the curtain! I said, 'how did you get in here?' He said, 'thru the window.' I noticed it was broken. My landlady always told me to keep my door and my one window locked - which I always did. This time it didn't do me any good!"

(Jim) "Why was he there?"

(Ursula) "He wanted to reminisce about old times – about how wonderful they were, and how sorry he was that it all turned out the way it did, and he really wanted me back. He said, 'let's have a drink!' I said, 'I don't want a drink!' I had a bad feeling – him being there. I told him, 'I have never forgiven you for what you did to me. You brought me into a strange country without knowing the language, and you kicked me out on the street!' He said he was sorry – he had tears in his eyes. So then he pulled out this bottle, which looked like liquor, and poured it in little glasses. He said, 'come on, pick it up, we'll toast!' I said, 'I don't wanna drink that stuff.' He said, 'yeah, you're *going* to drink it!' I said, 'Rudy, just leave me alone, there is no chance that we are ever going to get together again -- I'm done with you. You hurt me too bad! On account of you I almost took my life. I lost everything I had – everything I brought from Germany – and then you threw me out in the street!' Then he got loud and said, 'I told you, I'm sorry - I told you to forgive me! Pick up your glass and drink it!' I said, 'I'm not going to drink it, I don't wanna drink nothin with you!' So he picked up the glass, and said, 'you *want* this!' I said, 'I *don't* want it!'

Then he grabbed me and took the little glass and put it up to my lips. I clenched my teeth together, and he pushed the glass so hard against my teeth, that the glass broke. He forced my mouth open a little and forced a few drops into my mouth. I swallowed a tiny bit – I couldn't help it! It wasn't enough to kill me though. My mouth was bleeding. He said, 'if I can't have you, nobody else will!' We were struggling, and I began to scream. My landlady normally was not home at this hour, but fortunately she was then. She knew I never had anyone in my apartment - there never was any noise from my place. I only had a tiny little radio which I sometimes played music softly. She knew immediately something was wrong and called the police. I don't know how long it took – it seemed to me they got there pretty quick. He tried to kiss me, and hold me.

Then the police arrived. The chief, to whom I was familiar, came himself. He said, 'Ah, I'm so happy, Ursula, that you are all right!' I had showed my bosses a picture of Rudy before all this happened, because I was afraid of him. I told them that if this man ever comes around, let me know. He apparently came several times in the evening, watching the flower store where I worked. I guess he followed us, as my bosses took me home every night."

(Jim) "Do you think he really loved you, and do you think that this was a suicide pact for you both?"

(Ursula) "I know he sincerely loved me at one time, but I don't think so at this time. Now, he wants us to get together? He didn't want any one else to have me, and I didn't have anyone else at that time. I believe that if I would have drunk it, he would have too, as there were two glasses. I know it in my heart. It would have been a double suicide. He wanted to toast me and wanted me to toast him. It was about a pint sized whiskey bottle. He had to know that I would not go back to him – he knew me like nobody else did. Years later he again went back to Germany, and contacted my parents. He said he could not live without me, and he needed to see me and talk to me. He wanted to know if I was married, and how many children I had, and if still married. This was after I was married and had Stephen, my first child."

(Jim) "Let's go back to when the police came."

(Ursula) "They arrested Rudy and put him in jail. I don't know what happened to the bottle, because there was a big struggle and the bottle ended up on the floor. The police took the two glasses, with the liquid still in them and had it analyzed – it was cyanide! I don't know how long he was in prison or where. After he got out, he made many trips back to Germany – always stopping to see my parents. My mother was impressed with him. He was well-dressed and would take her shopping and buy her flowers and candy. She was always impressed with material things."

(Jim) "Hadn't you told your parents what Rudy had done to you?"

(Ursula) "No, I never wrote them about any of those terrible things that happened to me. My parents didn't know anything about me except that I had a job and an apartment and I was doing fine. Why worry them?"

(Jim) "So, what crime did they charge Rudy with?"

(Ursula) "I don't know – I got called one time to testify, but it was kind of a fiasco, because I didn't speak very good English. I really wasn't interested – he was out of my life, that's all that mattered. Years later, around 1974, just before my mother died, he visited my parents and told them that he had left America and returned to Germany. My mother wrote me and said, 'big surprise, Rudy moved back here and we'll probably be seeing him from time to time.'"

XIII

"I do not love you!"

(Jim) "How much longer did you stay in that apartment?"

(Ursula) "About a year and a half. Then I met an Italian man named, Criscuoli, through my boss' brother-in-law, Nick. Criscuoli was an American Airlines pilot. Nick said, 'I know a nice guy for you!' I said I wasn't interested. Between Nick and my boss, they kept working on me. Finally, I agreed to go out to dinner with him. He picked me up from work and took me to a health-food restaurant. It was so sterile – white walls, and big silver bowls with vegetables. I thought, 'where's the meat, where's the meat?' I was shocked to be taken to an ugly, boring place like this – it was like a hospital! I only knew a few English words, just being here about 6 months, so we had a real communication problem. I kept looking up words in my little dictionary to try to understand him."

(Jim) "How *did* you learn English?"

(Ursula) "My bosses took me to the movies several times a week – some movies, over and over. I put the gestures together with the sounds to learn the words. I watched my TV a lot and I connected the action with the words. My bosses then sent me to night school. The teacher thought I needed to go to an advanced class, but I couldn't keep up – that only lasted a week."

(Jim) "So, you and Criscuoli are hitting it off?"

(Ursula) "No, really, I didn't like him. It may have had a lot to do with the language - the dictionary routine was a nuisance. He really wasn't my type. I told my boss this. He said, 'give it a chance, go to a nice restaurant, where there's some music.' We did all that, and I guess he liked me, but I don't think he ever really loved me – maybe in his own way. I know I didn't love him. I was honest - I never lied. We saw each other for 4 or 5 months, and he asked me to marry him. I said, 'No, I can't do this!' He never touched me, never hugged me or kissed me. He held my hand once in awhile, but he never was intimate in any way. I didn't want him to make love to me, but some kind of endearment would have been nice. Not even a kiss on the cheek! That made me wonder - I should have been more suspicious. He told me he loved me and wanted me to marry him. I said (with help from the dictionary), 'I do not love you!' That's exactly what I said. He kept insisting.

You see, I was so alone. One day I said, 'if you still want to marry me, I'll marry you, and I promise you that I will be the best wife and mother I can possibly be, but, I don't really love you! Maybe later on, I can learn to love you.' I was a lot at fault here, because I was so lost. I had nobody to go to – no one to consult with. I couldn't go to my parents in Germany with my problems – what could they do? So he represented safety and security. He said, 'I have enough love for both of us. If you want to be my wife, I'll be honored and I promise you I will take care of you, and you will have everything possible I can give you.' He kept his word on the material things – to the day I got a divorce!"

(Jim) "So, did he provide for you?"

(Ursula) "We had everything - more than enough. God blessed us. If we had one thing, we had three. We didn't have one car, we had four! The more we had, the more he wanted - never satisfied! The man behind us built a swimming pool that was 40 feet long – well, we had to build one that was 44 feet long! It had to be bigger and better. There was never any satisfaction. It was very hard for me to live like that – all 28 years. I had so little in my life, and now I have every thing I wanted. It was so awful to have all those things - guilt feeling I guess. But what bothered me the most was that he was never satisfied – he always wanted more – and more! I was afraid that one day God would say, 'hey Criscuoli, I gave you all you have, and you are not satisfied – I think I'll just take everything away from you!' If he had a Cadillac, he had to have a Lincoln. So, we had a Cadillac AND a Lincoln. I had everything - our kids had everything. We lived in a large, beautiful, Spanish-style home

- with a bell tower! Then he talked about building another one! It hurt me that he never could be satisfied."

(Jim) "Did it seem to you that you were not able to make him happy, content, or satisfied?"

(Ursula) "I tried - I cooked, and cleaned, had his babies, and took care of them. That's all he was interested in. I just let him walk on me. I blamed myself for many things in my life, but for my marriage, I never did blame myself - no way. I don't blame myself regarding my children either. I know I was the best mother that it was possible for me to be - I know that. When each of my children died, I asked God, 'why, why?' But, I got to the point when my two girls died a few years ago, I could say to God, honestly, 'thank you for letting me have these two beautiful young women. And thank you that I could keep my promise to love them and nourish them through their lives.' That is what I promised them when I gave birth to them. When I stood at the graveside, I thanked God that I had always been there for my children. I was always there for my husband – unfortunately, emotionally he was never there for me! Only my children were there for me."

(Jim) "Where all did you live?"

(Ursula) "My husband piloted out of New York and we moved to Boston when he got transferred there and lived in a beautiful home for 12 years. He then was transferred to Dallas, Texas and we bought a house in a country club in Arlington, a suburb of Dallas. He was not satisfied with that, so he had a custom home built nearby. It was a large, extravagant home."

(Jim) "How did your husband treat you?"

(Ursula) "He never physically abused me, but he never was able to give of himself to me totally. For 27 years he called me nothing but a stupid German. After all that, you begin to believe it – you can't do anything right. He was Catholic, and having kids was what the church told you to do - you had to reproduce! I had to become Catholic in order to married him. Then, they didn't even let me go up to the altar – I had to stand down at the bottom of the steps. I could not believe this was happening! I had not been a Catholic - that's why I wasn't allowed up there for the special blessing. (Ursula begins to weep, as the memories rush back, reminding her of the humiliating treatment she received.)

We never had relations because we *wanted* to. We did it *only* because he wanted me to produce a child. I had a lot of physical problems and had a hysterectomy in my thirty's. That did it – we never made love after that! He told me I wasn't worth anything any more. I wasn't a woman – I couldn't bring children into this world.'"

(Jim) "You must have stayed pregnant all the time in those early years."

(Ursula) "Yes. I wanted about 8 children, I admit that, and so did he. I was excited – couldn't wait to get pregnant again! That was it. I was not worth anything any more to him after the hysterectomy. I should have known something was not right – that's not normal, just to have sex because you want a child. And then you don't sleep with your wife in the bed, but you sleep next to the bed on the floor. Something is wrong with that! I didn't have the courage to ask him about it. He so intimidated me, I was afraid to confront him about anything - he would start screaming at me. I was afraid of him! Now, today, I could stand up to him – but not then."

(Jim) "You mentioned that he had a bad temper."

(Ursula) "Oh, he had a bad temper, and nobody ever wanted to get that temper a'goin! He would scream at me – and the kids. He screamed all the time. If you wanted to talk about something that he found disagreeable, he would jump up from his chair - raise his arms, and shout. He was brought up by the old Italians, who are very emotional, dramatic, and loud. He did a lot of damage, a lot of damage to me – up here." (pointing to her head)

(Jim) "So, you had 7 pregnancies with him?"

(Ursula) "Yes, and lost two of them soon after childbirth. We had 5 live children -- 2 boys, and 3 girls -- Stephen, Kevin, Catalina, Latisha, and Monette. Catalina died at six months."

(Jim) "What about your parents back in Germany?"

(Ursula) "My husband flew my mother over here every other year. My husband liked my mother, because they were so much the alike. They went out early in the morning – and came home late at night with bags full of clothes, jewelry, etc.

We would pick her up at the airport, and when she saw me, there was no hug, no kiss, no 'I missed you.' She liked two of my children,

Stephen and Monette - none of the others. The children came to me and said, 'what's wrong with grandma?' I said, 'what do you mean?' They said, 'grandma loves Stephen and Monette, but she doesn't love us. She's mean to us!' She would give her favorite children chocolate, and not give the others any. That was typical, and difficult to explain. They would then torment their siblings with, 'grandma loves us more than you!' I went to my mother and explained that she shouldn't show partiality. What you give to one, you have to give to the others. She said, 'I'm going home, I don't need this! I said, 'that's right, you can go home! You have your ticket and everything, you can go home!' She fainted! Whenever she didn't get her way, she would faint. This was the first time she did it around me - I thought she was having a heart attack. We called the medics and they said it wasn't a heart attack, and asked if she had been upset about anything? They gave her something to calm her down. After that, when she fainted, I just walked away.

When I was in my early 30's, I took my son Stephen to Germany and I was pregnant with Kevin. My mother hit me, slapped me in the face! At 37, and she can slap me in the face? She said, 'oh, that feels so good - I just don't care for you!' I took Stephen and left. I called my husband back in the states, and related what happened, and he said to get a hotel. He asked if I wanted to go back there and I said, 'no, I won't go back to that house.' My father came home and asked, 'where's Ursula and baby, Stephen?' I don't know what she told him, but he contacted me and asked me to come back and he would talk to her. I told him 'no, I don't want you to. I'm 37 years old and will not be treated that way!' He cried. I said, 'I don't love her – because of the way she's treated me.' This hurt him very much."

(Jim) "What was daily life like back in Arlington, Texas?"

(Ursula) "We had big parties, with many guests – my husband liked to impress people! Once at the 'big house,' that's what I called the house in Arlington, we were having a party. Everybody had a drink in their hand, and somebody came by and handed me a bottle of beer. I held it out, acting silly, and someone said, 'hold that bottle out - I want to take a picture. You look cool!' My husband came by and slapped the bottle out of my hand and said I looked like a whore! In front of all those people - I was so humiliated! You could just hear a hush as the people were embarrassed. How do you apologize for something like that? I did apologize to some and they said, 'don't worry about it, we know what he's like.'"

(Jim) "Did he ever show you any affection?"

(Ursula) "The most affection he showed me, was to pat me on my shoulder and say, 'good job -- you did a good job' maybe after cooking a good meal or something -- like you would pat your dog and say, 'good boy!' That's why to this day, I don't like someone patting me on my shoulder – it brings back bad memories."

XIV

You gonna go see Elvis?

(Jim) "All this has been pretty traumatic, do you remember happier times?"

(Ursula) "Yes, let me tell you about a more pleasant experience. We were in Memphis once for my husband's ongoing training related to his airline piloting. We were with another couple and stayed at a wonderful hotel. Right down the street from our hotel was Elvis' home. Our friend, David, said, 'we need to go see Elvis.' I said, 'you gonna go see Elvis?' He said, 'no YOU are.' This is how it went. We had a bottle of scotch, so the deal was - if I got in there - I got the scotch! But, if I didn't get in - he got it! So we drove up to the gate and I walked up like a big shot. There were dozens of women around there. The guard said, 'What do you want? I said, 'I want to see Elvis!' He said, 'Yeah, I know, do you see all these women around here – they do to!' I said, 'but it's important that I see him.'

He really made fun of me, but that's okay - I was gonna win that bet! He said, 'No!' I said, 'I'm from Germany, and when I get back there I've got to tell them that I saw Elvis!' He said 'where in Germany are you from?' So I told him. He said, 'ok, listen, Elvis played handball this morning, and hurt his wrist - he's laid up. Would you like to meet his father?' I said, 'sure.' He said, 'ok, let me make a phone call.' So he made the call and set it up for us to go about a mile. I went back to the car and they said, 'you lost the bottle, you lost the bottle.' I said, 'no, I haven't lost it yet.' We went to the house - a plain house. They were having a party, and Elvis' father came to the door and invited me in. They were having wine, so he offered me a glass. I said, 'look, I really didn't want to break up your party, and I really didn't want to see you, I wanted to see Elvis.' He told me the same thing about Elvis hurting his hand, but 'you are very welcome to join the party.' I said, 'well, I can't do that - I have a carload of people waiting on me out there.' But, we sat down on the couch, and talked for half and hour. Finally, his new wife came and said to him, 'aren't you going to join the party?' She was kind of catty. That was a daring, fun thing. He gave me a life-sized poster of Elvis for my trouble!"

(Jim) "Who got the scotch?"

(Ursula) "After much laughter and joking, we broke the neck of the bottle and shared all around.

XV

I'm going to get a divorce!

(Jim) "So, you are in an unhappy marriage, but living large and having babies. I sense that in spite of his generous provision you were not happy, and looking for a way out."

(Ursula) "I got courageous. There appeared a lump in my breast, and I went to my doctor. He said, 'from what I can tell, it's not good.' He said 'let's do a biopsy tomorrow. Let me tell you, if I think its cancer, I'm going to take the whole breast – we're not going to mess with it. And, if I think the other breast is infected, we'll take that too.' I didn't feel good about this. I went home that night, and kept thinking about everything. I said to myself, 'if I ever do one thing in my life on my own – if I have any guts, I'm gonna show it, I'm going to get a divorce!' I got the yellow pages out and picked out an attorney. I called and asked him, 'do you make hospital calls?' He thought I was going to die and needed a will. He said, 'yes, I do.' I said, 'can you come and see me?' He was there in an hour – wouldn't you know, I picked one that had just graduated from law school!"

(Jim) "So you got a lawyer to 'practice' on you!"

(Ursula) (laughing) "Yeah, yeah, and he got rich on me. So, he came to the hospital, and was surprised to find out that I wanted him to represent me in a divorce. It took two years to get the divorce! Criscuoli was always gone, so they couldn't serve him the papers – always out of the country. He didn't want the divorce, so was avoiding the issue. He didn't think anything was wrong with us! He was some sick puppy to think that. My children were all still at home – basically teenagers."

(Jim) "What about the surgery you supposed to have?"

(Ursula) "They removed the lump in the hospital and there was no cancer, anywhere – that was good! I really got brave then! I came home after 4 or 5 days and gathered my children together to announce that I was getting a divorce from their father. Kevin said, 'why did you wait so long?' I said, 'it was for your sakes – I did it for you guys because I wanted you to have everything anybody could have. I wanted you to have a good life. I wanted you to have two parents growing up.' My Kevin said, 'you didn't do us any favors!' He walked off in disgust. Monette cried – she was her father's favorite. She used that favoritism against her siblings whenever she wanted to. She was very upset and said, 'I just don't want to lose my dad.' I said to her, 'you won't, you can see him most any time.' He was stationed in Dallas at that time. Serving him the papers was the hardest part – he avoided it that for as long as he could. I felt sorry him, I really did. In his heart though, he must have known we didn't have a happy marriage."

(Jim) "Did the children have a good relationship with their father?"

(Ursula) "Not really – Monette was his favorite, but there wasn't a lot of affection there -- except when she was little. When he hugged Latisha, she always pulled away – maybe she felt the insincerity. Stephen never was close to him. Kevin tried to be close – tried to please him, but when it came out that he was gay, his father lashed out at him. He said that his boys were little 'queers' because Kevin liked to write poetry and read, and Stephen liked to cook. He wanted them to play football! He exploded and told the rest of the children not to even talk to Kevin. Stephen said, 'you can't tell me I can't talk to my brother - what's wrong with you? I can't even talk to my own brother?' I think that was the worst time – because he basically disowned Kevin. They got into a fight one Sunday afternoon and Kevin joined in. Stephen got beat up by his father!"

(Jim) "Were you attending any church at this time?"

(Ursula) "We were married in the Catholic Church in Brooklyn, and attended one in Boston, and when we went to Arlington we continued. Once, Kevin was invited to go on a retreat with a group of young people from a Baptist church. He came to me and said he wanted to go – I said, 'fine.' He said, 'it's a Baptist Church.' I said, 'that's no problem.' When he came back home from the retreat, he said he had a wonderful time. He said, 'I accepted Jesus!' I said, 'you did?' He said, 'yes, and I want to go to church every Sunday!' I said, 'wonderful!' And he did. Every Sunday he would say, 'you gotta go to church, mama!' I hadn't been going anywhere – I didn't want to go back to the Catholic Church.

Kevin kept on, 'mamma, you gotta go with me to church!' And then the rest of the kids began to attend. I decided I would go just to shut them up! Even Criscuoli started going, and we ended up attending there for several years. He still went to confession at the Catholic Church at times. Once, when I talked to the pastor about how unhappy I was and would like us to have counseling, he refused to get involved. He admitted that he didn't want to 'rock the boat' with Criscuoli, because he was afraid of losing him. Criscuoli was a big contributor to the church - not for the right reasons, but for political and manipulative reasons."

(Jim) "So, let's go back to the divorce. How did that go?"

(Ursula) "His lawyer paid my lawyer off. That way I didn't get hardly anything. I got $17,000 out of all the stuff that we had. The judge couldn't believe what the lawyers conspired to do to me and leaning over his desk, grasped my hands and said, 'do you understand this, young lady, and do you understand that you get only $17,000?' Then he said to the lawyers, 'what's wrong with you gentlemen?' Then to me, 'Do you want to change this, young woman? We can change this.' I said, 'I understand, your Honor, I don't want to change anything.' He said, 'why not?' He was so frustrated! I said, 'judge, please let me get out of this marriage!' He said, 'ok.' I was so desperate."

(Jim) "Let me get this straight. The lawyer you found in the yellow pages made a deal with your husband and his lawyer to get you to agree with an easy divorce, which favored your husband?"

(Ursula) "His lawyer was a friend of ours – attended all our parties for years. He frequently made passes at me. I would just say 'get away' and make light of it, not to make the situation uncomfortable. When he found out about the divorce, he came on to me and said, 'Ursula, if you'll come my way, I'll get you anything you want! Otherwise you are going to get hurt.' I said, 'then I guess I'm going to get hurt."

(Jim) "Why did you not take the judge's advice?"

(Ursula) "I don't know... ... all I wanted was to get out of the marriage. I felt like I was about to lose my mind – I didn't know how much more I could take. My husband was about to kill me - emotionally. I felt I was in a desperate situation."

(Jim) "You got the divorce then?"

(Ursula) "Yes, I took the kids and moved out of the 'big house' into a rent house. Stephen was into his cooking career by then and was sent to Massachusetts. Catalina had died at six months of what they called, 'crib death.' Kevin was gone, so all I had left was Latisha and Monette.

So now, what was I going to do with my life? A friend said a doctor was looking for some help. He was an optometrist. I went to see him, and he hired me on the spot. Then he sent me to school to be an 'Eye-wear Fashion Consultant.' That's a big title – but it's just to pick out frames, and put them on someone's face! I got a degree – 'Eye-wear Fashion Consultant!' I did that for about 2 years – then he moved his business to Dallas. He told me he wanted me to go with him. I said 'no, I think I'm going back into my old profession, and open a flower shop.' So I did. I was in Garland, a suburb of Dallas, which already had five flower shops. I used the $17,000 I got in the divorce, and Criscuoli invested some of his money in the flower shop."

(Jim) "You mean your ex-husband put his money into your business?"

(Ursula) "He needed to shelter some of his money from taxes, so he put some of his money into my business each month. He still wanted me to come back, and this was his way of trying to manipulate me. Each time he came back from a flight, he came to my shop. One day he made this proposal, 'let's get married again, and you can do anything you want in the marriage, even if you want to have an affair (as long as he approved it!).' He wanted me back. His family had never had a divorce – and for Catholics that is a very bad thing. He was excommunicated from the Church, and that bothered him. He said, 'I know that you don't have much money, and I need to shelter some of my money. Let me put it in your business.' I said, 'well, you wanna be my partner – I don't wanna partner!' He said, 'no, I don't want to be your partner – just let me help you.' That was ok if he wanted to do that, so he did. But now he had that to hold over my head. He said, 'If I don't put the money in, you are never gonna make it - if I pull away, you are gonna be done for!' I had one designer working with me and one delivery person.

The last time he came to my shop, I could tell it was serious. He stood on the other side of the counter and said, 'we need to talk – let's go into your office.' I said, 'we can talk right here.' He said, 'I'm asking you again, come back to me!' I said, 'Criscuoli, that's never going to happen.' He said, 'make sure you know what you are saying!' I said, 'I know what I'm saying, I'm never going back to you! I don't want to be afraid again!' He said, 'you are going to be sorry! When I get through with you, you'll have nothing left.' And that's exactly what happened – he stopped putting money in it and I had to declare bankruptcy. I was not making that much money anyway. I had to let go my designer, and my driver – down to just me."

(Jim) "Did he pay you any child support or give you any financial help?"

(Ursula) "No, he gave me nothing. Occasionally, he gave the kids $100 each. He did my books... ….. he *fixed* the books. So, I don't know what happened to the money – I trusted him. But, he told me that day when I wouldn't go back to him, 'you are going to be sorry, when I get through with you, you'll have nothing – no business, no car, and no house!' That came true – they took my car, a beautiful Mercedes. A German friend of mine had gone to Germany and arranged to have mine shipped to me. I lost my rent house, because I couldn't pay the rent. He took everything I had. I didn't feel like a failure in my marriage, or with my children, but now I am a failure in business! I never should have accepted his money - I never should have let him do my books. You don't know how hard I worked to get that business off the ground. There is money to be made in the flower business, but here's my problem. A customer would come in whose loved one had just died, and they didn't have money for a casket spray. I'd say, 'don't worry about it - I'll do it for you."

(Jim) "Ursula, your heart is too big for your own good!"

(Ursula) "I know, I know, but I can't help it – that's just the way it is. I don't think God wants me to be any different than the way He has made me – I don't believe that!"

(Jim) "But, don't you think God would want you to sometimes say 'no' to people – for your own good, and maybe for theirs too?"

(Ursula) "I know it, but I have a hard time with that, I just can't bring myself to do that. I feel like I'd hurt people by turning them down."

(Jim) "I think that you have had a lifetime of being hurt by people, so that you are extra sensitive about what you might do to hurt someone else."

(Ursula) "You are probably right. Pastor Jim, *you* should have been a psychiatrist, you'd have made a lot of money! I'd have been the first one to call you!" (Laughing)

(Jim) (laughing) "And, I would have given you free treatments! I'd get my notebook out - have you lay on the couch, and listen to your problems. Then I would say, 'all right, that will be $200! Oh… …… you don't have any money? No problem, it's free today!" (Ursula convulse into laughter - one of the rare light moments in our recording sessions of her sad life - at least her life up to this point)

XVI

"Don't stop anywhere until you get to Texas!"'

(Jim) Divorce is very traumatic to many people - Ursula no exception. After a time of rest and recovery of a sense of well-being, we resumed our recording sessions. Family is very important to Ursula, so I begin to inquire about her grandson, Eli.

(Ursula) "Eli was my daughter, Latisha's baby. While living in Arlington, Texas, we got an anonymous letter from Iowa, addressed to Mr. and Mrs. Criscuoli, saying, 'if you want to see your grandchild alive, you need to come and get him – because he is being abused.'

My youngest daughter, 17-year old Monette, and a friend of mine went with me to Iowa. We drove into a horrible snow storm. Then we had to get the police and sheriff involved – it was a really bad scene -- getting that three-month old child."

(Jim) "Who was abusing him?"

(Ursula) "My daughter, Latisha - his mother. She was a drug addict. She got pregnant while living in Garland (we don't know who Eli's father is) and moved in with me for a couple months. Things weren't working out, so she took the baby and moved to Iowa with some guy. After I received the letter, I went to an attorney and he said, 'let me call the sheriff in the area where she lives. You go up there and find the sheriff and have him go with you to get the child out of that situation.' So, off we went. Latisha threatened me - said she was going to kill me if I took her baby! The sheriff told me to 'take the baby, get on the road, don't look back and don't stop anywhere until you get to Texas!'"

(Jim) "Why was Latisha so antagonistic towards you?"

(Ursula) "She never liked me – she was a very complicated child. She spent time in State institutions, and private hospitals. After my divorce, my ex-husband was still paying off some of the private hospitals. Nothing helped because she didn't *want* help. She could be a 'sweet-heart' - could be a wonderful woman, and the next moment she could tear your throat out!

Well, we got the baby. His head was huge! His eyes slanted upwards. I took him to a doctor as I thought he must be retarded. The doctor said the only thing wrong with him is extreme mal-nourishment. I took him to Pastor Ted at a local *Christian Church* and said, 'I need some blessings for this kid! I need you to pray for him like you have never prayed before!' Pastor Ted and the congregation prayed for Eli with marvelous results. So, I basically raised Eli from an infant."

XVII

Escape from Death – Again!

(Jim) "Did you have any other relationships with men after your divorce?"

(Ursula) "My daughter, Monette, told me once that her boyfriend had a plumber friend named John who wanted to meet me. I was very skeptical, but I did meet him. Eventually I found out that he was an alcoholic. He went into cycles – no drinking for six months - then he would go on a binge for three weeks. He showed up at my house about 9 o'clock one night. He acted kind of 'pushy' and strange, obviously under the influence.

He had been in Viet Nam several years, and through many discussions I had asked him if he spoke any Vietnamese. He said, 'not a word!' On this particular night, he went into the bedroom and came out with a handgun. He put his arms around me. There was a corner sink in the room, and he pushed me against the sink. He said, 'we're never goin' to be apart again – we'll always be together!' I said, 'what are you talking about?' I got scared! The dog went under the bed. John said, 'I'll never leave you again, I am so sorry I have left you so many times, I'll never leave you again – we'll always be together!' I said to myself, 'he is going to shoot me!' He said, 'before I die, I gotta do somethin'!' He then got on the phone. He had been estranged from his father and mother for many years. His father was a preacher and John had a very strict upbringing. They hadn't talked for many years. When we started going together, I told him he needed to be reconciled to his parents. Soon after that they got together and worked everything out – it was wonderful!

But that particular night, he said, 'I gotta do something.' I said, 'ok.' He goes walking toward the phone – talking Vietnamese – fluent! Fluent Vietnamese! Then he picked up the phone and called his dad. He tells him, 'good-by' and tells him how much he loves him."

(Jim) "Who is he speaking Vietnamese to?"

(Ursula) "Just to himself – he was off, he was already gone – I just didn't know what might happen next. I didn't know what danger I was in."

(Jim) "Did he have the gun in his hand?"

(Ursula) "Yes, all this time, waving it around. He hugged me again, and started talking that Vietnamese crap again. I said, 'what are you doin?' But, I could tell whatever I said was not working, ok? So at that instance, the phone rang. I don't know if it was his father calling back or his mother, I don't know that. But he put his hand on me and said, 'I'll get that phone!' He went to the phone, and I ran out the back door! I went next door to my neighbor, a black woman. I said, 'I have a problem!' She didn't asked questions but said, 'you need the police!' She called them and while waiting for the police, I called Sarah, a good friend of mine and told her the situation. She said, 'I'll be right there, stay out of that house!'

She was close, so it didn't take long. She said, 'let's go over to your house.' That's when I found out that the door was open about an inch. So we went in front of the door. John liked Sarah – she was a nice woman. She said, 'get behind me!' Then she said, 'John, this is Sarah. What are you doin'? Let me come in. She pushed the door open a little and he stood in the hallway with the gun pointing at her. I let out a scream and said, 'Sarah, he's gonna' shoot!' We ran away – that's when the police came. I was still standing outside when the police drove up – just one cruiser. They asked, 'what's the problem?' I explained it and they said, 'you ladies - go!' So we ran back to the neighbor's house. The police told the lady, 'make them stay there!' Immediately they had a SWAT team there.

They knocked on the door, but no answer. The door was still open a crack. They tried to talk him out -- without success. That continued for several hours. Then a police psychiatrist talked to him through the door. He said, 'we can talk this out!' John said, 'if you want me, you gotta come and get me!' Finally, they told him, 'we're coming in, John!' They opened the door and he was still standing in the same place with his gun fixed on them. They went in and there was shot after shot, after shot – bullets were just a'flyin.' Later, I counted 36 bullet holes in my house. They went nuts! Forensics told me later that one shot took John out. It was the kind that explodes on contact. He flew across the room. They shot my refrigerator – there were bullet holes all over my walls. There was blood on my ceiling, and on the walls. I had a large wall full of mirrors, all shattered."

(Jim) "Why did he do this, was he crazy, or drunk?"

(Ursula) "He was drunk. As I said, he went in cycles. Most of the time, he was a good man -- a wonderful person. He usually didn't get physical, but acted weird - talked stupid stuff."

(Jim) "Why did you waste your time on this guy?"

(Ursula) "I wanted to help him. We would talk a lot - but I never got to the core of his problem."

(Jim) "So, the swat team killed him?"

(Ursula) "Well, not completely. At this point he's still alive - barely. Then I passed out! They called two ambulances - one for each of us. He left first, then me in the next ambulance. He was in the emergency room when I got there, where seemingly hundreds of people were. This was a big thing! The police chief – and the media! I saw John lying across from me on a stretcher. I heard one of them, maybe the chief say, 'don't let this one die!' They knew they had done something seriously wrong, and was afraid he would die – putting *them* in serious jeopardy. Why did they put 36 bullets in my house? They killed him with one - what was the deal? He didn't resist arrest, although he still had the gun in his hand, he never did shoot it or move. Why didn't they shoot tear gas into the house, why did they have to force a confrontation? There are no good answers. The chief said they were afraid for their lives. But, when the one cop shot, and John went down, why keep shooting? That doesn't make any sense! The police department messed up – that's why they said, 'don't let this one die!' They knew they were going to have trouble. Unfortunately, I wasn't strong enough, or have enough guts to fight them. Today I would - today I would!"

(Jim) "What was your condition at this time?"

(Ursula) "All this extreme stress brought on one of my frequent epileptic seizures. It began in the ambulance, and continued at the hospital. They immediately took him up to O.R. and operated. They admitted me, and my doctor came. I wanted to know about John. She said, 'I'm going up to O.R. to see him and let you know.' They operated on him for several hours. She came down and told me that he didn't make it, he was too far gone.

They kept my house roped off for weeks. I could not get into my house because they were pulling up the carpet, repairing the walls, etc. The news media were constantly at my house, looking for a story or an interview. The initial story was in the newspaper, and on TV, but they were looking for me for follow-up stories, but I was in the hospital under an assumed name for protection. The police and the city didn't want the publicity. My Kevin went to my house, and three reporters jumped out of the bushes demanding information. He said, 'I don't know anything, I was out of town.' They learned I was in the hospital and loitered around, trying to get a story, but were not allowed into my room."

(Jim) "Why was the story so unique and in high demand?"

(Ursula) "I think it was because of how the police responded – shootin' up my house and all. We went to the police. I wanted some of my stuff replaced – things that they shot up. I talked to the chief. He said, "I'm very, very sorry that my men got nervous.' I said, 'what kind of nonsense is that – this was one dude, with one gun! You had ten dudes in front of my door!' My friend Mary said, 'we need to get an attorney.' Well, nobody would take a case against the police. They told me to get a civil lawyer. One lawyer told me to contact a civil lawyer in Washington DC and gave me two numbers. I called them and the first one said he would not touch the case. The second one said 'you want to sue city hall, and the police department. You are going to have to move out of state. If we get a conviction, you will have to leave Texas – are you willing to do all that? They are going to harass you til you die!' Arlington is not all that big – I didn't think I was ready for all that, so I let it go. Nobody did anything!"

(Jim) "Did insurance cover anything and did you move back into the house?"

(Ursula) "Very little. I went back after they replaced the carpet, fixed the walls, etc. but I couldn't stay there – not after what happened. It really tore me up – I was really sick after that."

(Jim) "Do you think that John was serious about killing somebody that night?"

(Ursula) "I'm sure he was – if somebody would have walked in that door he would have - yes he would have."

(Jim) "Do you think he would have shot you?"

(Ursula) "Yes, he would have – and then himself! I think he wanted to be shot. I really believe that at that moment – when he was standing in that hallway – he believed he was in Viet Nam! I believe that with all my heart. In his mind he was fighting the Viet Cong – that's what I believe. He went over the edge.

When they buried John, they tried to keep me away. I begged Mary, 'don't do this to me, let me go to the funeral, I'm going to be ok!' I begged and screamed and they finally let me go – I needed to get some kind of closure to this horrible thing. They had a closed casket. I told Mary, 'I just want to go to the cemetery - not the church for the funeral - just to watch the casket lowered.' She let me do that. Then I went back to her house and had an emotional breakdown. I looked at things different - not the same any more. I valued life more – I saw that in a blink of an eye, it could all be gone!"

XVIII

Ted – Love of my life!

(Jim) "Did you ever find true love? It seems that so far, you have not made the best choices in men."

(Ursula) "Yes! But, let me fill you in on the circumstances, which I believe were God-ordained that brought it about. After I lost my floral business. I went to work for Mary, a friend of mine in her flower shop. She was a wonderful person, always good to me. I gave my testimony at high schools and once at a Kiwanis Club. Oh, they honored me so wonderfully – they gave me a large, beautiful bell.

I once gave my testimony at an Arlington high school, and somebody told a member about it in Pastor Ted Caffey's church – First Christian Church in Grand Prairie, Texas. That person asked Pastor Ted if this Holocaust survivor could speak at the church. He said, 'ok, make arrangements for her to come.' So, it was set up for a Saturday night. It just so happened that he was not able to attend. I gave my testimony, and it was well received. The people said, 'why don't you come back to church in the morning and meet our pastor?' Another friend that had come with me, said, 'yeah, why don't we do that – I like this church!'

At that time, I was not attending any one church, only visiting around to various churches. Since I had been in Baptist churches for so long, that's pretty much the ones I visited. So the next day, we were there at Ted's church. He apologized for not being there the night before. He said he had heard wonderful reports of my testimony, and he was real pleased for our visit and invited us back. So, I did – I made that my church home. That was one of the best thing I ever did in my life!"

(Jim) Ursula's grandson Eli was a small child at this time and under her care. Once again, she demonstrates her great compassion and capacity for love, especially to those who need it the most and least capable of returning it.

(Ursula) "I had just gotten Eli, and this was when I took him to the altar for prayer. Much later, Ted told me that when I brought the child to the altar, he thought Eli was retarded – that's how bad that baby looked. I had a wonderful doctor for Eli that told me, 'his organs are not actually ill, all he really needs is constant care, good food, and love. You will be surprised at his recovery after you have given him that.' I said, 'you mean he's not sick anywhere?' She said 'no, but he probably has emotional scars, and will eventually need counseling.'"

(Jim) "You mean, at three months, he developed emotional problems?"

(Ursula) "Yeah, he was in a closet for three days, screaming – and his mother didn't even know where he was! I'm not going to tell you any more about that – it's just too bad. When he was two years old - I took him to a child psychologist in Dallas who handles abused children. He told me that we would always have problems with him. I spent a fortune on him. When he was a teenager, he went to Mental Health, Mental Retardation (MHMR) in Dallas. They helped him – they were good. Eli was a nice kid, but he always was alone, and he always felt nobody liked him or loved him. So, he did crazy things to impress people. In his heart, he knew I loved him, even though his grandfather didn't. To this day, we have a very close relationship. He is a lot like me – he speaks what he thinks – what you see is what you get. When he tells you something – you can take it to the bank!"

(Jim) "Where is Eli today?"

(Ursula) "He has made some very bad choices. He now is in prison. He's told me how very sorry about what-all he has put me through, and it will never happen again. I told him, 'if you are going to continue this way – you can't live with me any more.' That's his biggest fear. Actually, his biggest fear is of me dying! He said he doesn't know what he would do. When I go, my son Stephen will suffer in a different way – Eli will suffer loud. He is going to let everyone know that he is hurt! When he gives his word, he does everything to keep that word! Whether it's right or wrong, he keeps his word."

(Jim) "Let's go back to Ted. How did that relationship go?"

(Ursula) "Ted came to my flower shop one day and Sarah, who worked for me, told him I was home - seriously ill. He asked, 'why didn't anyone let me know?' He was the pastor of my church. I had been in the hospital, and released because they said they couldn't do anything for me, except increase my Phenobarbital and Dilanten – that was the medicine I was on for epilepsy. I had lost my balance – I couldn't walk, couldn't get up, or do anything. They said, 'just go home.' I thought, well, 'I'm gonna die now!'

Ted said to Sarah, 'I'll go see her -- how do I get in the house?' She said, 'the door is unlocked – just go in.' He came, opened the door and hollered, 'Ursula! It's Pastor Ted.' I said, 'ok, come on in.' He told me he had gone to the shop and found out I was home, sick. He said, 'we need to pray!' I said, 'ok' so he pulled a chair over to my bed. I was not even able to get out of bed. I distinctly remember, he had on dark pants and a white shirt, no coat. He sat on the chair and started praying, which was strange for him because his church and denomination didn't believe in healing by the laying on of hands. He'd never done anything like this before. As he was praying, I lay there skeptical, and thought, 'well, maybe I should close my eyes out of respect.' But, I really didn't expect anything to happen. I didn't believe in *anything* at this point in my life."

(Jim) "Were you not close to God at this time?"

(Ursula) "People told me, 'you need to pray, you need to pray, God will heal you, God will heal you!' God didn't do anything, ya' know? I still had seizures – and they had gotten worse. The older I got, the stronger the seizures got. All of sudden… …… I began to listen. It was as if the prayer was coming from a different county – far, far away. I didn't understand the words any more, but I heard Ted's voice. Now, I was nosey – I wanted to know why he was so far away! It was like it came from a different country. Then there was this heat coming into my body! I kind of wondered, 'what's that all about?' Then it started on my neck - it was like someone was moving furniture – that's the only way I can explain it. The pressure was on my head, over my face, down my neck – then back up - doing the same thing again. Over and over, three times. After three times it seemed like my body, starting at my feet, felt some strange sensations.

I had to look over at the pastor. He was lost in the Spirit, and his white shirt was so wet it stuck to his body and he was silent – almost in a trance! I said, 'Pastor... ......Pastor!' He then came to. 'Yeah, Ursula?' I said, 'I'm healed!' He said, 'I know! I know!' I said, 'Ok, let me get up?' He said, 'Where are you goin?' 'I'm gonna dump my medicine!' He said, 'don't you think that's a little premature?' That was his exact words. I said, 'what's wrong with you – you are the pastor, you should have more faith than me! I know I'm healed, I know I'm healed!' I had not been able to get up - even to go to the bathroom. I had had no control of my limbs.

I got up! I got my medicine from the night stand and he got up saying, 'don't fall, don't fall!' I said, 'I'm not going to fall!' I walked to the bathroom and dumped all my medicine down the toilet... ... and flushed! He really freaked out – his eyes glazed over. He was not really with it. I went back to bed. I said, 'you better sit down, too.'"

(Jim) "Did that cure you -- did you ever have any more seizures?"

(Ursula) "I had one more seizure, and that was the following Wednesday. I was at church - at a prayer meeting. I was sitting there, and started to feel funny. I said, 'I'm not going to have a seizure! I'm **not** going to have another seizure! I'm healed, I'm healed!' Then I thought, 'I better get out of here.' So I got up, and quietly made my way to the bathroom, saying, 'I'm healed, I'm healed!' When I got to the bath-room, I hit that floor, saying, I'm healed, I'm healed!' That was the last words I spoke. I believed it in my mind. I hit that floor so hard! That was the last seizure I ever had! Last seizure! I knew I was healed - there was no doubt in my mind. When something like that happens to you, you gotta believe, you gotta believe – otherwise you shame God. That was a miracle, what happened to me! I started having seizures after coming out of the camp at age 11 and they continued for 29 more years – that was hell! I have been free of epilepsy for 38 years!"

(Jim) "So, then did the seizure stop right then or go through its normal cycle?"

(Ursula) "The pastor knew something was wrong, because I nor-mally didn't leave the service to go to the bathroom. He sent one of the ladies, and said, 'please go check on Ursula!' She went in and found me. I always had tongue depressors with me. They were taped all over my house, in my purse, inside my sleeves – taped to my arm – because the seizures were so bad that I needed them close. Everybody knew about that, so when she found me on the floor, she ran back and said, 'I need some help.' Somebody came and assisted. It was a really bad one – wet my pants and all that kind of stuff! But, that was the **last** one, thank God! 38 years of freedom from seizures!"

(Jim) "Were you passed out – unconscious?"

(Ursula) "Yes – the real bad ones I passed out - others I didn't. Most of the time I knew what I was doing, I knew I was peeing, but couldn't stop. I knew I was drooling, and making all these noises, but couldn't stop. That's the worst part – being awake and not able to do anything about it. You know what you are doing, and you can't stop yourself! That was why I was always glad if I passed out – then I didn't feel anything. I didn't put energy into trying to stop it, so afterward I was not as exhausted. I usually ended up in the hospital after seizures – to spend the night and go home."

(Jim) "Did you share your testimony of the Holocaust and your healing of epilepsy to individuals or groups?"

(Ursula) "Yes, I was invited to speak at various organizations. We belonged to a lay-ministry mission through the Baptist Church, and I shared my testimony at various places. Many people came to me from different churches and said how ashamed they were because they had epilepsy. They even had their medicines delivered in brown paper bags to keep it a secret."

(Jim) "Did this healing of yours change Ted's ministry?"

(Ursula) "His whole preaching changed! People in his church asked, 'Ted, what happened to you? Your preaching today – that was really solid.' In their mind, they thought, 'something must have happened to him.' He was an excellent preacher from the head, but when all this happened to him, it totally changed - his heart was now in his preaching. You could tell by just listening to him. And he even looked different when in the pulpit – because his heart was filled with joy! And when we prayed – just Ted and me – we prayed for the Holy Spirit."

(Jim) "So, how did you and Ted know about the Holy Spirit?"

(Ursula) "I had heard about it, read about it, but he'd heard about miracles and all but just didn't believe in it. But he saw a miracle, right before his eyes – he knew how I had suffered with seizures. Sometimes I couldn't go to church because I had a seizure the night before – you don't want to be driving the next day! Sometimes I had 3 or 4 a week, and the older I got – the worse they were."

(Jim) "Did the doctors believe they started back at the concentration camp?"

(Ursula) "Blows on the head – scar tissue. I know I don't have any scar tissue now, I know! I know when God did it – He moved everything around in my head and fixed it all!"

(Jim) "Did your relationship with Ted change after that?"

(Ursula) "Ted was in an unhappy marriage for years – his wife rarely came to his services, and he was the pastor! There were a lot of problems there. When I had my shop, Ted would come in occasionally. He played the guitar, and sang beautifully. Sometimes when we worked late, like on holidays - Mother's day, etc. he would come and entertain us with his music. I could tell that he really gave me too much attention. I didn't know his wife, but I was not about to break up a marriage. Truth be known, though, no one can break up a marriage - if it is solid. You can stand there naked and it won't affect you because you know what you have at home – and you are strong in your relationship! I didn't know that then – otherwise I would not have left the church, which is what I did. I went back to the Baptist church, because at this point I really like to go to church. He didn't leave me alone, even though I was going to a different church. One day we just had to have a talk. He told me how he felt. I said, 'don't tell me all that – I don't want to hear it!' Well, he got a divorce, or more correctly, his wife got the divorce.

One day, Ted took me with him to his church leadership committee meeting. He said, 'I want you to be there and hear what's being said, so nobody can say afterwards that something else was said. He told them that he wanted to resign. They said, 'why, pastor, why?' He said, 'because I don't feel right, being your pastor – as a divorcée. He said, 'I don't believe in divorce!' They didn't want him to resign. He was good to his people, and an excellent preacher! He was still their friend, even after he left the church he was invited back to all their socials.

So, Ted continued to come to see me, and eventually we planned a small wedding. I had lost my flower shop, and was working at Mary's shop. She did all my wedding flowers, and it was lovely, lovely, lovely! We had 50 close friends – they knew what we'd been through. It was a wonderful wedding in the First Christian Church in Arlington. The pastor's wife at that church told me, "Ursula, with all the weddings we have had, our church never looked that beautiful – flowers everywhere!"

(Jim) "After leaving the pastorate, what did you and Ted do?"

(Ursula) "We ministered in nursing homes in the area, as well as other ministries. But, one year after our marriage, Ted had a stroke! It was at the Cerebellum part of his brain, which is the stem of the brain, so the doctor thought he could be rehabilitated. He was doing well, walking with a cane, standing erect and getting back his abilities. Exactly a year later he had another stroke, and that took him down, not only physically, but mentally in some ways.

He went to Parkland Hospital in Dallas – spending 8 months there. He lost his eyesight and speech – he was in bad shape. The personnel at Parkland (a large community hospital) were wonderful – they saved his life - they really did. Then he went to Baylor Hospital in Dallas for rehab. His speech improved, but that's about all. Mentally, he got better and was pretty sharp, at least for awhile.

We then moved Lancaster, Texas, another Dallas suburb during which time he had mini-strokes. We began using Hospice – then he was on morphine – a bad time!"

(Jim) "How long were you married?"

(Ursula) "Seventeen years. One year after we married he had his first stroke, and he suffered from that for 16 more years. In the beginning, he talked to me, but lost that ability – then they sent us speech therapists. Hospice was there about 8 months. The lady from Hospice said that she had never seen a body that had been in bed 15 years, and not had bed sores. She said, 'his skin looks like a baby's bottom – real smooth.' It's because I kept him clean. I cared for him – rolling him over every two hours, night and day! I set an alarm clock for the night turnings. I moved a futon into his room for me to sleep on to be close to him as he was in a hospital bed. I also got him a bell that he could ring if he needed me. Once every two weeks, Hospice sent someone over so

I could go grocery shopping, get my hair done, or whatever I needed to do. I never wanted him to be alone, so I got back as soon as I could."

(Jim) "What kind of man was Ted?"

(Ursula) "He was a very extraordinary man! He taught me many things – even during his convalescence. I never thought in my whole life I would be a widow – it's such an ugly word! When you are a widow, you don't belong anywhere, your friends are uncomfortable, because they are all couples – you don't know where you fit. It makes you an outsider."

(Jim) "Did you share with Ted your past experiences?"

(Ursula) "Yes, as time went on, we had many conversations which resulted in my emptying my heart to him all the events of my life. He was so empathetic and touched by my stories. Our love grew as we shared our lives, holding back nothing. It was so freeing to have a man love me so deeply and unconditionally. I had been so disappointed and disillusioned with men in my life that I was almost to the point of believing that I would never find someone like Ted. The joys we experienced as we shared our past lives moved us to ecstatic love. We were soul-mates!

I'm glad that I had those years with Ted – I wished I had more – but that was not to be! But, I still have him with me – and I don't regret one minute of my life with him! He was the most outstanding Christian I have ever met, and I have met some nice ones ….. and I have met some bad ones!

The day before he died, the strangest thing happened. I was in his room basically all of the time, crocheting. All of a sudden he turned his head over to me – with real clear eyes – he had the most beautifullest blue eyes. He said, 'come and lay with me a little bit Ursula.' I said, 'ok.' I laid on his electric hospital bed - my head on the pillow. He said, 'lay your head on my shoulder.' So, I did. He looked at me right in the eyes, real clear, and told me how happy I had made him, and how much he wanted to thank me for the years I had given him of my life. He said he was sorry that we couldn't make the life together that we planned. He felt bad about that. He told me a whole bunch of stuff. After all that was said and done, he closed his eyes, and turned his head over to the other side. That was his good-by to me - I knew it! When I saw how clear he looked – totally normal. His face was normal, his eyes were like they had been – bright, brilliant blue! He rallied a little bit the next day, and at 9:30 that night he went to heaven!

With Ted, for the first time in my life I was completely and unconditionally happy - and loved! I lost everything when I lost him. Ted was such good man – he was such a good pastor. People would call him at 3 AM because their mother was admitted to the hospital, etc. – and he was there. He was always there for his people. He had never been sick a day of his life – never even had a cold! I didn't understand why I had to lose him."

(Jim) "Ursula, think about those years that you had with him. He not only gave to you unconditional love, but you were able to give to him unconditional love. That's a treasure trove of wonderful memories that no one can take away from you!

Were you and Ted able to attend church during those 15 years?"

(Ursula) "I had a van, left from my flower shop, the only thing I didn't lose. I had a wheelchair lift installed on it for Ted. We used that to go to church for awhile, but eventually we stayed home. We prayed together, and read the Bible. I read a lot of Christian books - some were brought by the Hospice people. They sent in a grievance counselor, who was also a pastor. She came about 3 times a week to see me, and sometimes she took me to lunch. She told me about God and gave me material – including good books."

XIX

My Monette is gone!

(Jim) Ursula's years with Ted had been glorious, in spite of the health issues. It is my experience that we are brought together with our spouse in care-giving due to health issues in a significant way that usually doesn't happen during times of busyness, career, raising children, and home-making. Giving of ourselves to our loved one involves sacrificing our own pleasure and agenda. This is fertile ground for the seeds of love to germinate and grow. But, Ursula's care-giving and losses are not over at this point.

(Ursula: "After Ted passed, I was so devastated and felt all alone - so empty. I felt like part of me was gone – which it was. I needed to move, there were too many memories in that place. My daughter Monette and I grew very close then and she was so supportive at the time. We moved to Bedford, Texas where I worked in a flower shop. After a few years, Monette moved to Bogota, in northeast Texas and asked me to come with her. At first, I experienced a time of depression, loneliness and emptiness. But, it was there that I started to seek God like I hadn't done in a long time. I began to attend a little church across the street in which I was the only white person! The people were so nice, friendly, and caring.

I met a woman there named Mary that became my friend. She came to see me every day at noon - brought food, and prayed with me. She had a truck which she used to pick up food, package it, and distribute it to those who needed it. She would encourage me, telling me that no matter what comes in life, God is always there. With her influence,

I felt myself being drawn back to God, and got progressively better in many ways. We did this for a whole year. I could walk to the church, just across the street, but she insisted on picking me up. I knew that years ago she had cancer, but had been fine for five years.

Regretfully, I noticed in her behavior that she was pulling away from me. I didn't know why. One day I asked her if everything was all right, and she said, 'yes, everything is okay, baby.' She always called me 'baby.' One day she came and we had lunch. As she was leaving, she opened the front door and hugged me. She said, 'You don't need me no mo, baby!' I said, 'What are you talkin' about?' She said, 'You okay, you gonna be just fine. I gotta go. I gotta go to somebody who needs me now!'

'You don't need me no mo?' I was just crushed, because she didn't give me any explanation. Her son told me later that she went home and went to bed... ... and never got up. The cancer had just eaten her up - she never told anybody. She was the most beautifulest woman I ever met in my life. She was a jewel. Years earlier her husband had been an alcoholic and went to prison. He sent word that he wanted Mary to come see him. She went to see him, took him a Bible and told him to read it, it would straighten him out. She said, 'I don't want to see you until you straighten up,' and didn't until he did straighten up and eventually he changed and became a wonderful man. That happened many years earlier. At her funeral there was standing room only. Many people shared how Mary had affected their lives.

God brought her into my life, and through her, my relationship with God was restored. When she said I didn't need her anymore, I didn't understand. But, that was her way of saying, 'good-by.' At noon every day, I really missed her, as that was when she always came. I still miss her. I believe she saved my sanity – with her genuine Christianity and her strong love. She pounded it into me. She said, 'you better listen, baby!' And I did. She was my pathway back to God. Her son was the pastor of that church, a wonderful man. Soon after that, when I moved away, Mary's daughter came and helped me pack and clean the apartment. Good Christian people!"

(Jim) "During this time are you are living in the same town as your daughter, Monette?"

(Ursula) "Yes, and one day she came to my door crying. I said, 'what's the matter, Monette.' She said, 'look at my arm!' She had a huge lump on her left arm. She said it just came up overnight. She had always been healthy, did aerobics, and was active. I took her to the doctor immediately. He said, 'I don't like this - let's get her to the hospital and do a biopsy. I knew something must be bad. It was cancer, which had started in her breast and spread all over. We moved her to a nursing home in Paris, Texas because she was going down so fast. I really didn't want that, but after the doctor recommended a facility, we checked it out. It was very nice, with caring staff. They gave her four chemo treatments, and at the fifth one the doctor said, 'no more.' We said, 'what do you mean, no more?' She said, 'I can't help you any more.' Monette jumped up and said, 'I'm goin' to die?' She hadn't thought it had been that serious. The doctor said, 'yes' and walked out of the room! I'm not a violent person, Pastor Jim, but I wanted to hit that woman. She was so rude! That doctor from the cancer center had no compassion, no empathy, no feeling. Monette was so devastated – screaming and crying. Then the nurse from the center came running and put her arm around her and comforted her.

We took her back to the nursing home, as there was nothing that could be done for her recovery. I had moved out of my rent house in Bogota when Monette entered the nursing home and they supplied me with a cot and a couch close to her. Monette said, 'mama, don't leave me alone - you'll come back, won't you?' I told her I would. I was all she had - her 11 year old son had moved back with his father in Waco, Texas when she got sick. I took her shopping every day, if only just to buy a pair of earrings. That was good therapy, as it kept her mind off her illness. One day the nurse said, 'it won't be long, she probably won't last after today.' The doctor promised that she would not suffer. He kept his word. All the staff knew she was slipping out - tending to her throughout the day as she gained and lost consciousness. Residents in wheelchairs came to say good-by. I crawled up in bed with her, and a nurse got in on the other side. I had my head leaning on hers, and said, 'I love you, Monette!' She opened her eyes and said, 'I love you, mama!' 10 minutes later, it was all over."

(Jim) "It was good that you could be with her at this special time."

(Ursula) "Oh, I don't know what I would have done. There was nothing that could have kept me from being with her. It was such a beautiful moment... ... when she said, 'I love you.' The staff was so wonderful, I couldn't repay them. My Monette is gone, my Monette is gone! It's so mind boggling - she had never been sick, and five months later she's gone. But, I never let go of God, okay? I prayed and prayed, really hung on. 'God, give me the peace that I need.' And He did. I never left her those five months. Through prayers, laughter, keeping a good attitude and just being together, we can go through the toughest times.

I made all the funeral arrangements. She said she wanted a white casket with a pink stripe around it, and a pink lining. I went to the funeral home in Bogota where the manager knew Monette, and told him what she wanted. He said, 'no problem.' It was the power of God that held me together. I ordered a large supply of flowers. As a floral designer, I was able to get them wholesale. I made the most elegant, most beautifullist casket spray you've ever seen. I told them, 'get me the most cheerful flowers you have - no sad ones.' They were the most brilliant, colorful flowers! Those at the nursing home treated me like someone real special -- so compassionate. 5 months of caring for me and my daughter, followed by the funeral and my moving out – they were wonderful."

(Jim) "Did you move back to Bogota?"

(Ursula) "Yes, and that was hard. I had already lost Ted, and six other children, and now, my Monette! She was only 43 years old. My other daughter, Latisha, who lived in Waco, Texas, came and spent 2 weeks with me before Monette passed, and later came back for the funeral."

(Jim) "How was Latisha's health?"

(Ursula) "This is really going to be hard to tell you, Pastor Jim. She had emphysema with a permanent tracheotomy. She was doing pretty well, as far as I knew. I talked to her on the phone one day, and she didn't sound quite right. The next evening at 9:00 I got a call from her estranged husband. He said, 'she's gone!' I said, 'what, what are you talking about?' He just kept saying, 'she's gone.' I said, 'who, where is she gone?' I thought she maybe left the nursing home where she was staying. I was so frustrated. He said, 'she's gone, she died.' I said, 'how?' He said, 'I don't know' and hung up. He's scum, and I mean scum! After

I hung up, I called the nursing home and asked, 'what happened to my daughter?' They got the supervisor on the phone and said that Latisha came to the desk at 4:30 PM and said she couldn't breathe very well. So, the nurse told her to go into her room, and she would come and give her a breathing treatment. The nurse got in there right away and gave her a treatment and left about 5:00 PM. The nurse came later to check on her and her tracheotomy had been pulled out, laid on the table…… … and she was dead.

I have never gotten over this, Pastor Jim. I never believed that she pulled it out herself. I think somebody else did it. She wanted too much to live! I was distraught - I had just lost Monette five months earlier. I would have liked to have it investigated, but it was not practical as I lived 5 hours away. Maybe she did it herself, but I don't believe it. Maybe I don't want to believe it. It's so hard for me to believe that she did that."

(Jim) "Was there family members there - any care-giver? No one to crawl up in her bed and be with her for the final moments as you did for her sister?"

(Ursula) "That's what bothers me - I was not with Latisha. I was with Monette all the way, and now Latisha is all alone – no one to really care. Her son, Eli, was in prison at the time, and still is. I felt so helpless!"

(Jim) "What you must do is accept the fact that there was nothing you could do. You cannot blame yourself. You can only do what you can do."

(Ursula) "See, I blamed myself, and probably still do. I sent her money every month for incidentals, like candy. Her husband wouldn't give her a penny, so I sent it to the nursing home and instructed them to let her use it as she needed it."

(Jim) "I know you have always been close to Eli. Tell me more about him."

(Ursula) "He never used or sold hard drugs, but he smoked pot." He and a friend got caught selling stolen goods. He got 10 years, but you know, they usually cut that in half. He has changed a lot. Hopefully he will be out in a few months. I get letters frequently from him, and he tells me he reads his Bible every day and attends church regularly. I know Eli, so I believe he has really changed. He and I are very close and when he gets out, he will come and live with me. He is a brilliant, wonderful person- a good kid. Well, he's 31 now – not really a kid. He says he's going to wait on me hand and foot. You know, Pastor Jim, God's grace has always been over me!"

(Jim) "Tell me about your friend, Charlie."

(Ursula) "One day, about 10 years ago while living in Bogota, Texas, this man named Charlie was at the local grocery store. Seeing a lady with many bags of groceries, he offered to help her home with them. She happened to be my roommate. He saw me reading and asked if I liked to read. I said, 'I love to read!' So in a few days, he showed up with a box of books. We began a solid friendship based on a mutual respect and understanding that we would take nothing from each other. Soon after this, because of his situation, he moved in with me and we have maintained this friendship where he is there for me, and I am there for him. Charlie has had many heart-aches in his life, and I guess we are good for each other. We read God's Word and pray together regularly. God's grace has supplied our needs over and over."

(Jim) "How has churches and individuals ministered to you and blessed you?"

(Ursula) "Oh, my goodness, I have been blessed so many times by so many people. My church paid my electric bill, which had accumulated to over $1,300. I can't count how many people have been there for me, from sitting with me in the hospital while having stints put in my heart, or bringing groceries and home-made meals. I have received beautiful clothing, and flowers (oh, how I love flowers!). As much as I needed and appreciate all those things, what really means the most is the love and friendship so many have expressed. I feel so blessed that there are brothers and sisters in the Lord that have opened up their hearts of love to me."

(Jim) "Who do you have left of your family?"

(Ursula) "All I have left is my oldest child, my son Stephen, and my grandson, Eli."

(Jim) "Ursula, you've had one blow after another almost all your life!"

(Ursula) "Yes, but God has always been faithful. Sometimes I've been completely overwhelmed, and think that I can't take any more, it's too much. And then God just puts me on His lap and then I know, whatever is next, I can handle it. That's the way it's been for 78 years."

XX

On the Lighter Side

As I look back on the three years we have known Ursula, I remember the many times she has graced our home with her sweet affection for my wife and I. She has shared meals with us, and been with us for small group fellowships, where she has brought everyone to tears as she shared her testimony. Since she does not drive, we have picked her up for church, taken her to doctors, shopping, etc. We have taken her to give her testimony where the audience was mesmerized by her story. One thing you can always depend on if she comes to your house. She will find a way to bring a fresh flower arrangement even if she has to get a taxi to take her to buy the flowers! Her career as a professional floral designer, her German culture of floral importance in society, as well as her appreciation for the beauty and creativity of flowers have all contributed to her passion for flowers. Usually she would include one of her awesome German recipes - a desert or German potato salad.

The Washing Machine

Ursula's life story tends to be quite heavy, so I've decided to relate a story that brings some comic relief, as well as help you understand our relationship with her. She never converses with me on the phone or in person without inquiring as to "Miss Lois." Concern for my wife reinforces Ursula's unselfishness and compassion for others. The following story may not have been humorous at the time, but looking back it seems to prove the old axiom, "No good deed goes without punishment."

One day, about six months into writing this book, I discovered that Ursula was making huge monthly payments on a washer and dryer, which was limiting her funds for groceries, rent and prescriptions. I asked her to have them picked up as they were on a lease/purchase plan which still had a considerable amount left to pay on for her to own them. In checking around I found a good looking used set for a reasonable amount at a used appliance store. I installed them in her laundry room and noticed that one of the rubber "feet" on the washer was missing. Oh well, I leveled it up the best I could and left. On the next wash day Ursula called me in a panic. "Pastor Jim, you've got to come, this washer is jumping all over my laundry room!' Well, I drove the ten miles and operated the machine for a few minutes, and sure enough, it had a full load and was vibrating and jumping around So, I searched around town and found the rubber foot, adjusted everything so that it was level and left believing the problem solved.

Next wash day: "Pastor Jim, this washer is out of control and it's a war zone in my laundry room!" I returned to listen to Ursula's story: "I was washing a load of clothes, and the washer started dancing around the room. Charlie (who happened to be there) got his arms around it, trying to keep it steady and hold it down. Well, the vibration in the walls caused some canisters full of flour to work their way off the shelf next to the washer and tip over onto Charlie's head! He is still hanging on. What a sight, 10 pounds of flour all over him, the washer and the laundry room. He's still hanging on – not good, because the bread-making machine on the next shelf then vibrates off, falling on Charlie's head! Ursula says, "I think he has a concussion!" Fortunately, he was all right.

So, I loaded the washer and dryer **back** into my truck and took them back to the dealer. He gave me my money back, and as I was leaving, I said, "lets plug in the washer and you can see how it jumps around." He says ok, so I plugged it in and set it to the spin cycle. Would you believe that it didn't move a single bit? Since it was on a concrete floor, he concluded the problem was not with the washer, but Ursula's rent house *floor*. So, I repaid him the money, loaded up the machines again and took them back to Ursula's. Upon inspection of the floor - sure enough, it was pretty much rotted out, and not stable enough for this older washer. Evidently the newer, rented machine had a better stabilizing mechanism.

Well, I have too much invested in this project in money and time to give up now! Stopping at the lumber yard, I picked up a couple bags of concrete mix. At home, I built a form the size of the washer base. I mixed the concrete, poured it in the form and then leveled it at 4" thick. The next day, after the concrete had set up good and solid I went back to Ursula's house. Moving the washer out of the laundry room, I then brought the concrete base (very heavy) in on a dolly and locate it next to the dryer. Then I wrestled the washer back and up on its new foundation. In the process, I hit my head on a sharp shelf bracket causing the blood to flow nicely down my forehead. This didn't really bother me that much, as that was no big deal, but it was very upsetting to Ursula, who has a very tender spirit. The washer still vibrates a little, and its 4" higher than the dryer next to it, but as Ursula says, "it's just fine, Pastor Jim, it's just fine!"

"Sweetheart Banquet"

This February, 2013 we celebrated Valentine's Day at our house. Members of the Sunday School class that I teach were invited to this wonderful catered event. When I picked Ursula up, she was dressed elegantly, and as usual, a vase full of beautiful flowers arranged by the 'master's' hands. The catering people served us through all the courses, and wouldn't you know, Ursula was flittering around, filling tea glasses, etc! She seems to be in her element when serving, loving, and sharing. Mysteriously, the roses she brought, which usually lasts a couple days, lasted two weeks! She couldn't believe it when I told her.

XXI

Forgiveness is Freedom!

(Jim) "So, where are you today in your spiritual walk?"

(Ursula) "God is my buddy, my friend, my father - my everything!" I try to live the right way. I still feel love for people, and enjoy reaching out to help in small ways. I struggle with physical issues, but God has never left me. I've just had cataract surgery on my eyes, and I can see so much better now! He is who I will continue to trust, for whatever challenges lie ahead. Some would say that many times I have been a victim, and that's true in a way, but I never *considered* myself a victim, but a **victor.** I have overcome by the grace and power of my God."

(Jim) "In an overview of your life spiritually, it seems that you had a visitation of God at the river when Jesus put His hand up as if to stop your suicide attempt. You attended a number of churches along the way and it seems you had an encounter with God due to your relationship with Ted, which led to your healing of epilepsy. But, was there any time that you believe that you had a genuine born-again experience?"

(Ursula) "Yes, back in Arlington, Texas in the 70's. I attended a revival meeting on a Saturday night where the congregation broke up into sharing groups. The idea was to be transparent, and pray for one other. I ended up with a one-on-one with a woman whose husband had fought in World War II. She was so full of hate and in that setting, she broke, emotionally. She lashed out at Hitler, and unexplicably, to *me*! She said, 'Hitler killed all the Jews, but he lacked one..... YOU! I was totally blown away at this outburst - it didn't make any sense. Why was I the target for all that hate? I tried to reason with her, but she was, at that point an emotional basket case. A pastor or leader, I don't' remember who, began to deal with her - talking and praying.

I thought to myself, 'this woman is so full of hate and un-forgiveness - that's incredible!' Then it hit me – the truth. It was like God said to me, 'Ursula, *you* are guilty of the same thing. You have un-forgiveness toward all those who have mistreated you!' I fell on my knees and prayed for God to forgive me and to help me to forgive others......and there were a lot of them! You know, Pastor Jim, the hardest one to forgive was myself! That's the day I really got free. That's the day I believe Christ became my personal savior and my sins were totally forgiven. The next day was Sunday and I was back at church. I was asked to give my testimony of what had happened the day before. Something came over me and as I was sharing, boldness came over me and an ability to speak to the people as God gave me the words. I then gave an altar call, which was a strange experience for me, and people came forward to seek God. The husband of the woman who lashed out at me the day before was the first one to the altar confessing that God had done a mighty work of grace in he and his wife. That experience taught me how devastating un-forgiveness is, and how powerful God's forgiveness is as it was working through me."

(Jim) "Ursula, what message would you like to leave with our readers?"

(Ursula) "I would like to remind our readers that no matter what the circumstances, no matter what goes on in your life, don't ever give up! Keep your faith in God, even if at the time you have trouble believing. God has blessed me all my life, and I consider my biggest blessing to be the privilege of living in the United States. I love this country with all my heart. I will never, ever forget where I've been - daily reminding myself what I've been through, and will never take my blessings for granted."

Conclusion

During the process of relating her life story to me over the last 3 years as I dug deep into her memory bank, Ursula has run the gamut of emotions. She justifies the cost to her physical and emotional well-being with the hope that this book will accomplish several objectives. First, the reader will develop a deeper understanding of God's unconditional love by noting that He never forsook Ursula, even in spite of her immense suffering. His deliverances and healings are evidence of His divine intervention and grace. Second, the reader will acknowledge that every time Ursula was brought to the brink of surrender, God intervened and blessed her with courage and determination—helped her see that she wanted to live, to *survive*. Third, the reader will recognize that the Holocaust was one of the most heinous acts perpetrated on humanity in all of history. The story of this godless time, in all its dark detail, needs to be told to today's generation and to future generations. As the late philosopher and scholar George Santayana states, "Those who cannot remember the past are condemned to repeat it." We must never forget.

Lastly, due to lapses of judgment and poor decisions she made along the way, Ursula suffered the consequences accordingly. Good judgment can be said to stem from bad judgment. A lifetime of heartbreaking lessons taught Ursula this firsthand. Dear reader, oh that the stories told throughout this book help influence your decision-making process. And may God's wisdom, obtained only through His word, guide you along a more enlightened path.

Ursula's challenges today are no less traumatic, as they involve her health, finances, and family. It may be easy for you to think that all her torture, disappointments, and times of facing death can be laid aside, and as someone may heartlessly say, "just get over it!" But, you didn't go through it, I don't have the nightmares about it – she does. Remember, in this life, memory is a blessing AND a curse!

In closing, I would like to relate how that writing this book and knowing Ursula Caffey has impacted my life. Sometimes when experiencing something painful or devastating in my life, I compare it with what she and others went through, and then conclude that my problems are really nothing at all. It is rare to meet someone who was a part of such a significant historical event like the Holocaust. When in Jerusalem about 20 years ago I visited the Holocaust Museum. The news articles, displays, and memorials sobered me like nothing I had ever experienced. I could not even speak to anyone for some time after exiting the grounds. It is unbelievable to think that in my lifetime such inhuman cruelty could have happened. Now, years later, crossing my path comes someone who was there who personally experienced that horror and survived to tell about it. It goes without saying that Ursula was destined to live through it, and the grit she developed as a 11-year old sustained her through many more tests and trials. She even came to the brink of abandoning her survival determination on the banks of the Hudson River at age 21. If not for the hand of God in that cloud a precious life would have been snuffed out. Because of that Hand, there is **this story**.

Dear reader, do *you* see that Hand? It may be stopping you … … or it may be beckoning you … … … …

Final Word

At 10:00 AM Sunday, June 16, 2013 Ursula answered a beckoning call from Heaven. Her Lord and Savior, Jesus closed the earthly chapter of her life to begin a new eternal chapter that is totally free of torture, pain, fear and sickness.

"I have fought a good fight, I have finished my course, I have kept the faith: Henceforth there is laid up for me a crown of righteousness, which the Lord, the righteous judge, shall give me at that day: and not to me only, but unto all them also that love his appearing." - 2 Tim 4:7-8

www.ingramcontent.com/pod-product-compliance
Lightning Source LLC
Chambersburg PA
CBHW051425280526
45785CB00003B/1170